the cats... a lot more took french. at 8

Thursday.... Fine weather flogg'd 2 men wit
Simons and Williams caught. Dr ordered Simons" in
taken from his legs on account of Swellings, Capt.
them kept on, Requested to go on shore, Shattuck
Could not go, at 4 Supper at 8 Reported

Friday,.... Fine weather employ'd at Sundries
12 dinner went on shore, at 5 PM Knight ran
from the boat, taken a general fight, during the
he stabb'd a Native in the Small of the back wi
Knife, at 9 returned.. So ends to day

Saturday... Fine weather, 20 Whalemen in the
harbour, 1 outside, Court on shore Sentenced Knight to
a fine of 50 dollars and receive 100 lashes on the back
at 4 Supper at 8 Reported, heard that he had not a far

Goat Island and Northwest extremity of
Juan Fernandez

BEYOND WORDS

This is number _____ of the 2011 Bancroft Keepsake

for Friends of the Bancroft Library.

Each is well-bound with a distinct paper: Rives, Ingres, Fabriano & Arches. And each has it's distinctive marbled linen cover. Slow night! — . .

The energy of what the summer holds in store is already becoming manifest. Phonecalls & letters from west coast re: the co-ordination of readings & exhibits. A letter from Ruth in Wales re: her possible visit to America & a jaunt through Hopi-land with me. Shaws recent visit, of course. That energy of "seeing" the cosmos through our mutually-shared "G" eyes, our flavored madness, our quest to translate archetype–symbol–landscape into poem–paint–song–& sculpture etc. Certainly I was given great input by our trek into the canyons around Navajo Mtn: Long, Dowizhebiko, Tsegi, Keet Seel. The night in Long Cyn, especially: I remember deep sexual crevasses of sheer brick-colored canyon walls — & the triangular–green black–cedars

below them. And — oh — the sky — a translucent indigo sheet of glass all night long — moving in front & behind the red cliffs — loaded with stars, a neat red/blue penumbra created under the near-full moon

Thus, I would like to consider what I absorbed that night — as a theme for a future painting: "Night in Long Canyon" — or "Night Above Dowizhebiko." Cedars, cliffs, sky — & music. ————

BEYOND WORDS

200 Years of Illustrated Diaries

Susan Snyder

Heyday, Berkeley, California
The Bancroft Library, University of California, Berkeley

The John Muir diary appears courtesy of John Muir Papers, Holt-Atherton Special Collections, University of the Pacific Library. ©1984 Muir-Hanna Trust.
The Jabez D. Hawks diary appears courtesy of the Society of California Pioneers, San Francisco, California.
The William Otis Raiguel diary appears courtesy of the Environmental Design Archives, University of California, Berkeley.
The Ayako Miyawaki diary appears courtesy of Miyawaki Mihoko-san and the Toyota Museum of Art, Toyota, Japan.
The Kim Bancroft diary appears courtesy of Kim Bancroft.

Library of Congress Cataloging-in-Publication Data

Snyder, Susan, 1948-
  Beyond words : 200 years of illustrated diaries / Susan Snyder.
     p. cm.
  ISBN 978-1-59714-164-2 (hardcover : alk. paper)
  1. Diaries--History and criticism. 2. Drawing--Themes, motives. I. Title. II. Title: 200 years of illustrated diaries. III. Title: Two hundred years of illustrated diaries.
  PN4390.S69 2011
  809--dc22
                              2011002755

Cover Art: William H. Meyers; frontispiece, John Brandi; pages 4–5, Yoshiko Uchida; page 7, Heinrich Biedermann; pages 148–149, Susan Snyder; page 151, William H. Meyers.

Cover & Interior Design/Typesetting: J. Spittler/Jamison Design

Beyond Words was published by Heyday in collaboration with The Bancroft Library, University of California, Berkeley. Orders, inquiries, and correspondence should be addressed to:
        Heyday
        P.O. Box 9145, Berkeley, CA 94709
        (510) 549-3564, Fax (510) 549-1889
        www.heydaybooks.com

Printed in China by Imago

10 9 8 7 6 5 4 3 2 1

pull Leiko on her skates
and I can hardly take him for
a walk because he pulls
me and runs so fast.

Mar. 12, 1932.
    Brownie is awfully sick he's been
sick for a long time. We were
going to put him to sleep but Mrs.
Harpainter is taking care of him
and is doing Christian Science.

Mar. 16, 1932.
    Poor little Brownie he died today
he had so much fits. He was almost
ten months old.

BROWNIE
DIED
MAR. 16
-
JULY 19
TEN MONTHS
OLD
1932

For journal keepers

 Contents

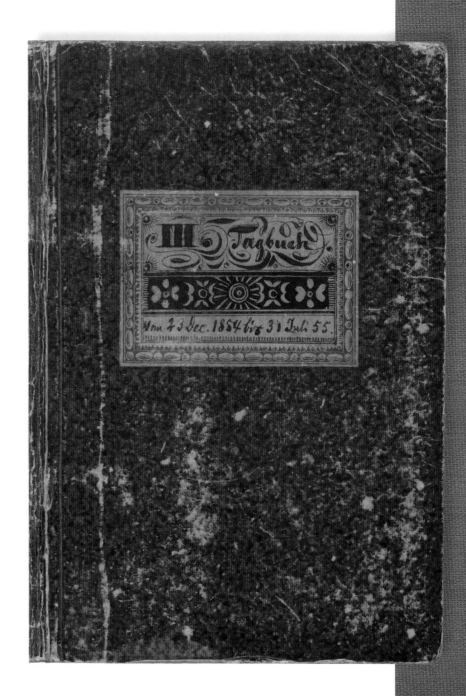

Acknowledgments

Thanks to Kim Bancroft, Maria Brandt, Peter Greim, Cana Hasegawa, Maki Owen Hasegawa, Jessica Lemieux, Ben Madley, Mihoko Miyawaki, Jenny Mullowney, Marc Selvaggio, William Wagner, Kunio Yoshitani; California Historical Society: Tanya Hollis; Environmental Design Archives, UC Berkeley: Miranda Hambro; Heyday: One and All; Oakland Museum of California: Robin Doolin; Society of California Pioneers: Patricia Keats; Holt-Atherton Special Collections, University of the Pacific: Trish Richards; The Bancroft Library: Anwaar Al-Zireeni, Jamie Bardwil, Kristin Bietsch, Terry Boom, Randal Brandt, Marjorie Bryer, Amy Croft, James Eason, Charles Faulhaber, Kenna Fisher, Peter Hanff, Dan Johnston, Lorna Kirwan, Lauren Lassleben, Dana Miller, Teresa Mora, Michele Morgan, Theresa Salazar, Neda Salem, Mary Scott, Elia Shelton, and Daniel Wikey.

Introduction

From the time when the first personal diaries we know of were written by Japanese court women in the tenth century, people have marked time, distance, sequence, and discoveries in their diaries. They have recorded indelible truth by creating maps that mark the milestones of geography and life itself, fixing experiences, thoughts, and feelings into the ink and onto the paper of protected volumes. Journals are compact and modest, yet they are vast and deep, containing the lives that keep them. And when diarists work drawings, doodles, decorations, and photographs in amidst the words describing a day's events, they greatly enhance the capture of that day. ❧ The union of text and illustration makes for journals that call to mind what words or pictures alone cannot entirely encapsulate. Vivid detail is the key to description, and drawings provide dimension often lost with words. Born of introspection and outward observance, illustration lends verisimilitude to the outrageous and unthinkable as well as the mundane. And with truth comes beauty: the pages of these resplendent journals become works of art, with style and composition. They are like priceless miniatures, focused and concentrated glimpses into times and places long past. ❧ Attempts to recover the past in large and general terms will not persuade anybody that it was lived by human beings. The past was lived by individuals, and their intimate diaries can be invaluable to historians, supplying the rich cinematic particulars of personal experience not otherwise available. Journals do not transcribe reality, but create an authentic common language with which we understand each other's lives. ❧ The last two hundred years have seen a growing flood of vernacular autobiography. The first flow was thanks to a general literacy, and blogs, social networking, and gossip columns have taken us to full torrent. These are all about individuals taking stock, telling stories, pursuing perspective, "following my fancy," as Paul Gauguin said of his writing, "following the moon." Our attempts to distill great quantities of information into a rich elixir of truth and meaning recall Virginia Woolf: "Nothing has really happened until it's been recorded." ❧ Non-diarists may cry "tedium" or invoke busy-ness. They may fear discovery or see their own lives as unworthy of careful observation or what others might call obsession. But people *do* keep journals for as many reasons as there are diarists. Writing can be a mechanism for coping with misfortune or hardship, a way to honor memory, a means of entertainment or exercise for the mind, an aid to concentration, or a haven for quietude and order.

Keeping a diary is a way to live with intention or to pose and chatter. There may be therapeutic and creative benefits to keeping track of where one is, one day at a time. It is a way to remember and a way to define one's life, a clasp-locked legacy, something to leave behind. In a diary one is free to express prejudices, unpopular opinions, and unspoken longing. Diaries may or may not be secret or private, but they always offer their writers the opportunity to be intimate, honest, self-conscious, and aware. For Anne Frank, perhaps the world's most famous diarist, her diary was a friend: "I haven't written for a few days, because I wanted first of all to think about my diary…paper is more patient than man…and now I come to the root of the matter, the reason for my diary: it is that I have no such real friend." ❧ Canadian artist Emily Carr wrote, "Ah, little book,…you help me to sort and formulate thoughts and you amuse me, which is more than housecleaning does." ❧ American novelist Joan Frank acknowledged "the sensuous pleasure of the act of writing itself—as journals open and close, pages are filled, and innumerable, passionate letters appear and dissolve, like imploring faces in a window." ❧ And Joan Didion wrote in 1966, in *Slouching Towards Bethlehem,* "Keepers of private notebooks are a different breed altogether, lonely and resistant re-arrangers of things, anxious malcontents, children afflicted apparently at birth with some presentiment of loss." Later she adds, "I think we are well advised to keep on nodding terms with the people we used to be, whether we find them attractive company or not. We forget all too soon the things we thought we could never forget." ❧ Along with the reasons for keeping a diary goes the question of for whom. Writing and drawing for one's own eyes only can yield a tidy volume that will help to shape thoughts and opinions, to get it right, to figure it out, to shelter and brighten one's own vital spark. It can be an exercise in self-definition. Sometimes people have written in the hope that their pages will be read by families or friends left behind, the next generation. Some of the diaries in this collection were compiled for presentation, some as research notes, and some, with posterity peering over the shoulder, for eventual publication. Several of these are shelved alongside other versions, showing in the succeeding transcriptions that perceptions were selected and stories edited, perhaps absolving the writer of culpability or excising disparagement of others. ❧ The diary takes many guises and entices us with features—it may be bound in leather or vellum with red satin ribbon page marker, or a handmade paper wrapper, or it may be a commercial calendar book, indigo-edged with brass lock and key, perhaps with a fancy title page and fashionable preprinted multiple choice questions and tidbits of inspirational wisdom on the daily entry pages. Calendar book diaries come with handy maps, time zones, almanacs, the year-at-a-glance, address lists, and glossaries. Commercial formats offer a structure to lighten the onus of expression and help to create a routine. Lines and dates relieve the pressure created by a free-form blank page. ❧ Many diaries on our earth have been lost, discarded, or destroyed. Relatively few survive to be read, deciphered, and savored by subsequent generations. And many of those volumes that have found their way into archives and museums are damaged, showing the ragged stumps of knifed-out pages and expurgated entries; diarists who decide to make their pages public sometimes don the mask by purging the perilous parts of their past, but page stumps and ink blots also tell tales. ❧ Most of the diaries chosen for this book are in The Bancroft Library at the University of California at Berkeley, where I work, trolling the ranks and ranges of collections. In acid-free boxes, arranged on shelves in temperature-controlled darkness, they have come as donations, tag-alongs, bequests, purchases, or hotly contested auction lots. They have been selected by librarians to fill in the chinks in the house of history, to put a name and face to a time and place, to supply humor, pathos, grime, existential angst, and vision to the entirety of the human record. Hubert Howe Bancroft was a great believer in the validity of the personal and humble view, so it is appropriate that his namesake library now houses a magnificent assortment of journals, spanning several centuries. Once in a while a diary is called up into the light of the library reading room by a researcher who wants to listen to a voice from the past, or who needs to see from an individual perspective, or who is curious about the mind meanders of a particular person. Often bland, worn, and featureless on the exterior, the diaries glow with an unforgettable illumination when viewed historically. It is the diaries that speak the loudest in the empty library at night. ❧ In his introduction to Virginia Woolf's *A Writer's Diary,* Leonard Woolf said he believed it was usually a mistake to publish extracts from diaries because "the omissions almost always distort or conceal the true character of the diarist." This book takes that risk in order to display illuminated diaries as works of art. The contours and lines of words and drawings form a landscape, a visual invitation to memory and reflection. These stories of others, unknown and familiar, are of lives worth knowing. They are our stories, and they are beautiful.

" Often bland, worn, and featureless on the exterior, the diaries glow with an unforgettable illumination when viewed historically. It is the diaries that speak the loudest in the empty library at night. "

Pedro Font

MARCH 28–MARCH 29, 1776

Father Pedro Font's journal records the second Juan Bautista de Anza expedition, September 29, 1775–June 2, 1776, from San Miguel de Horcasitas to San Francisco and back, conducted by order of Viceroy Bucareli for the settlement of Monterey and San Francisco. Plotting their locations with an astronomical quadrant and measuring their daily distances by his own steps at a marching pace, the science-loving padre was disgruntled by the lack of a decent compass. He was eager to advance, and one suspects he was a bit dissatisfied with the delays associated with a large group of "people, pack mules, and saddle animals," though they frequently covered twelve leagues, or about thirty-six miles, a day. He was much taken by the beauty of San Francisco Bay, the "Harbor of Harbors, a marvel of nature," guarded by two "very high perpendicular cliffs"—white on one side and red on the other. He drew the entrance to the bay, "Plan de la Boca del Puerto de San Francisco," as well as the Farallones, Angel Island, and San Bruno Mountain in the journal. He noted that they could see the tops of great redwood trees from what is now San Mateo, and that they were entertained by local Indians "with singular demonstrations of joy, singing, and dancing." Though Font's brain must have been buzzing with all the calculations that he kept, including tree measurements and tidal activity, he made time to comment on many of the sights they encountered and the accepted theories about them. ❖ Font made corrections and additions to what is known as his "short diary" before it was transcribed into this lavish version immediately after his return to northern Mexico.

llado mas delo que esperaban enel recinto de estas Lomas, cuya estension será de unas 3 leguas. En ellas, y en sus cañadas encontraron mucho bosque, y leña, mucha agua en varios mantiales, ó Lagunas, bastantes tierras de pan llevar, y enfin muchissimo pasto en todo el terreno: de mo do q. puede lograr la nueva poblaz. mucha leña, agua, y zacate, ó, pasto pª Cavallada todo cercó, y solo le faltan maderas pª fabricas grandes, aunq. pª Jacales, y barracas, y pª estacada del Presi dio hai bastante palizada en los Vosques. Icon una corta providenz. q. se dá, se pueden lograr las maderas como las quisieren; pª desde unas 6 leg. mas allá del Arroyo de Sn Josef Cuperti no hasta unas tres leg. mas acá del Arroyo de Sn Fran.co sigue un llano como de 15 leg. q. le llaman el llano de los Robles pr estar mui tupido de ellos, y de todos tamaños, del q. se pue den sacar mui buenas maderas. Mas de esto, desde la cercania del Arroyo de las Llacas sigue hasta la punta de Almejas una serrania mui alta, lo mas de ella tupida de Pi nabetes, y otros Arboles, los quales llegan hasta la Cañada de Sn Andres, de la q. hablaré mañana, y de estos parages se puede sacar la madera quanta se quisiere de todos ta maños, y no con mucho trabajo, pª la saca no está mui dificultosa. Los Indios q. bi mos en el Camino desde Monte Rey parecen mansos, y de buena condicion, y muj Po bres, y pr lo desarmados q. se presentaron no dieron muestras de belicosos, ni mal intencio nados; y los q. habitan en las Cercanias del Puerto son bastantemte barbados, pero en el color se distinguen de los demas.

Dia 29 Salimos de la Laguna, ó mantial, en donde nace el arroyo del Puerto alas 7 y q. de la ma
96. ñana, y á las seis y media de la tarde, paramos en el Arroyo de Sn Mateo, haw. caminado unas 15 leg. pr el rodeo q. hicimos, y Doi á decir, pº desde el Puerto á dho Arroyo solo habrá unas 6 leg. largs por el camino recto. Con el motivo delo q. se registró ayer, determinó el Sr Co mandte salir del Puerto, dando buelta á las Lomas q. lo cercan en las inmediaz. de la Boca, y seguir su playa inter. hasta salir á la tierra llana, pª lo q. despachó la Requa pr el Camino recto con orden de q. parase en el Arroyo de S. Mateo, y cogi. nosotros distinto Rumbo, caminamos como legua al Este, una al Estsudeste, y una al sudeste, y llegamos á un hermoso Arroyo q. pr viernes de Dolores le llamamos el arroyo de los Dolores. Desde un altito observé aqui el Rumbo del Puerto pr este Viento, y vi q. su estremo caia al Estsudeste, y q. un Pinabete mui alto, q. de mui lejos se divisa descollando como una gran torre, en el Llano de los Robles, y está á la orilla del arroyo de Sn Fran.co cuia altura medi desps caia al sudeste. Caminamos como tres leg. mas con Rumbo al Sur, al Sudeste, y Oeste al ultimo, dando buelta á las Lomas hasta salir al lla no, y encontramos con el Camino, pr el q. andubimos un poco con Rumbo al Sudeste. Aqui de terminó el Sr Comandte pasar á registrar una Cañada inmediata llamada de Sn Andrs q. está en la Serrania de Pinabetes (q. tambien llaman Palo colorado) y remata en la punta de Almejas, con el fin de ber si tenia buenas maderas pª la Poblacn del Puerto. Por lo q. de jando el Camino, caminamos como 1 legua corta al Sudoeste, y algo al Sur, y entramos en dha Cañada, en la q. bimos siguiendola mucho bosque, y con mucha palizada, y varia de buena madera, Encinos, Madroños, Pinabete, y tamien Alamos, y otros Arboles, y mucho Vare
Jon

MAR DEL SUR

Escala de dos leguas Mexicanas.

> *The indians whom we saw on the road from Monterey appear to be gentle, good natured, and very poor; and judging from the lack of arms which they evidenced, they gave no signs of being warlike or ill intentioned.*

Francis Phillips

SEPTEMBER 8, 1813

Encased in a hand-sewn skin cover with a burned-in admonishment, "Secret," the ship's log "Remarks &c. H. M. S. Racoon" is believed to have been kept by the ship's clerk, Francis Phillips. Phillips and his fellows set sail from Spithead in Hampshire, England, and traveled by way of Madeira and Rio de Janeiro to take possession of Astoria, Oregon, and its lucrative fur trade from the Americans in 1813. After two damaging, embattled months in the estuary of the Columbia River, the *Racoon* sailed to San Francisco for repairs, where it lent its name to the deepwater channel between Tiburon and Angel Island, Raccoon Strait. From there, the ship's log keeps up with stops in Hawai'i, Tahiti, and up and down the coast of South America before the voyage home to England in 1815, "staggering into Plymouth Sound, the old ship labouring hard and cracking like a cotton stick into port." Phillips ruminates on diverse subjects during his shipboard hours, including war and popular literature. The voyage was arduous and included the challenges of a weather-damaged ship, a gunnery accident that killed eight of the crew members, and long stretches without going ashore. Rations were so short that Phillips took to shooting pigeons for food in the Juan Fernandez Islands, the location of the ship when the pages reproduced here were inscribed. Previously frequented by pirates and used as a penal colony for Spanish criminals exiled from the mainland of Chile, these islands were at Phillips's time known primarily for having been home for four years to the sailor Alexander Selkirk, the inspiration for the novel *Robinson Crusoe*, which Phillips mentions in the log. ❧ Sometimes, as a reference for future passages, ship's officers were encouraged to sketch anchorages, landfalls, distinctive features of coastlines, and dangerous areas—perhaps this was part of Phillips's inspiration.

Remarks &c &c of Bacon Cumberland Bay falling in with Cremies squadron and anticipated compensation we shall derive from the capture of the american establishment in the River the latter we were most sanguine of not only the pleasure of doing honor to the British arms in so distant a part of the world but of the ...

Juan Fernandez moored with the Stream Anchorage Cumberland Bay 40 fms poor anchorage

The Island of Juan Fernandez Lat. 33°4'S Long 78°32' Var 12E
Taken from the Anchorage

This is the Island Captain Vancouver anchored at in the same Bay on his voyage round the world in the Discovery Sloop of war also where the noted Alexander Selkirk dwelt 4 years in solitude from which the well known amusing Novel called Robinson Crusoe was derived. this place is inhabited (now but very lately so) by Spaniards who are transported from Chile for different crimes they are about 500 in No. this Island from nature is beautiful and would produce any kind of vegetable Corn &c if the Spaniards was not so damned lazy & would cultivate the ground there was plenty of Bullocks & sheep which we got 6 Dollars a Bullock & ... for a Sheep there was some Turnips & Strawberrys growing wild ...

> *This island from nature is beautiful and would produce any kind of vegetable. Corn, &c if the Spaniards was not so damned lazy & would cultivate the ground. There are plenty of bullocks & sheep…there are also some turnips and strawberrys growing wild.*

Thomas Pickstock

OCTOBER 23–OCTOBER 25, 1824

> *...entered Grand Bogue Creek at ¼ to 11 o'clock, it was quite calm, passed the mouth of turnoff lagoon...by ½ past 12 o'clock; alligators' lagoon resembles that of manatee; navigation intricate, and a family was lost here for a week.*

Thomas Pickstock left pages blank in the beginning of his large and comprehensive journal in order to preface it eventually with a detailed index to its contents—names, places, topics, and events. While a soldier in the British army during the Napoleonic Wars Pickstock traveled throughout Europe, but even after Napoleon was finally defeated, he could not contain his wanderlust and left England once again, in 1816, to sell British goods in Belize. He eventually visited Honduras and Guatemala during a time of great political upheaval, and finally the United States and Canada on his route home to England in 1829. A writer possessing a beautiful hand, Pickstock was also an accomplished watercolorist, painting on his diary pages views and maps of islands and keys in the Gulf of Mexico. He seems to have intended his diaries to be read, for he gives reference to works for further study by "the reader" who wishes more detail. In this section, he describes the circuitous waterways and life among the keys and reefs of Belize in 1827. In other parts, he notes observations on Central American Indians, agriculture, and slavery and includes a plan for his dream house with a store on the ground floor. Pickstock also used his journal as a copybook for his official correspondence and included consular letters of passage. ❖ Inscribed on the frontispiece is "The careful clerk, if wise, should never think of any arms but such as Pen and Ink." Art critic John Berger wrote, "We who draw do so not only to make something observed visible to others but also to accompany something invisible to its incalculable destination." The daily entries and the gentle landscapes, like gems in settings of prose, must have created for Pickstock a sense of normalcy and regularity in an existence that could not have been easy or predictable.

middle of the N.W. side, I took up our Quarters at Jacob Mustaais, its 40 miles from Belize thro' the Turneff and elevated above the Sea 20 feet in its highest parts.—

The Schooner Phænix was seen over the Land coming thro' the Creek with Mess.rs Alexander France, Captain Arrowsmith, Turnbull, & Earl, the last has been some time at Belize selecting mahogany for his London connexions.

Wednesday 24th Octr.

The Schooner Phænix does not appear, and we argue that the Gentlemen who had started in another Boat, must have returned to Belize, probably as their Schooner was not fit to cross the Channel as it was rather rough Yesterday.—

A Brig from Jamaica in sight proves to be the "Foundling" & the Pilot Abrahams goes on board to take her into Belize. Pratt & Vernon two other Pilots, are here, looking out for Vessels expected to arrive.

At 5 pm the Phænix came in with Mess.rs France, Arrowsmith, Turnbull, & Earl, they had gone thro' the Lagoon & anchored at the Calabash Keys last night.

Thursday 25th

Rather blusterous & rain in the night, I went to Saddle Key four miles distance in a Boat with Two of our negro Boys, this Key

SE   Bearing about one Mile   NW Side

Long Key   Hat Key   Saddle Key   Eastern Sandy Bank

Hat Key.
off S. side bearing SW from Long Key.

Hat Key.
SW. by W about a Mile.
It is smaller than Saddle Key, four young Cocoa Nut Trees upon it,—high Mangroves in its centre. Broad Leaf Trees, & the Tea Box intermixed with the creeping Samphire.

Long Key NE about 2 Miles.

Saddle Key
bearing NE about one Mile

South view Saddle Key, 4 Miles from the Light House, bearing SSE.
There are Seven Cocoa nut Trees upon this Key, Black tight, or Broad Leaf Trees, Tea Box, Mangroves & very thick with the Samphire, very low & innumerable pelican nests thereon.

William H. Meyers

OCTOBER 7–NOVEMBER 8, 1843

"Went on shore…found my dear M. in tears… I now feel really attached to her, after having passed the afternoon with her, had a trying scene—bade all farewell."

Career sailor William Meyers adorned the margins of his elaborate three-year journal with coffins when crewmembers died, and the flags and colors of all other ships encountered at sea. A gunner on the USS Sloop-of-War *Cyane* in the Pacific Squadron during the Mexican-American War, Meyers was a stickler for ship discipline, gleefully reporting all onboard infractions and their resulting punishments. Most of the watercolor paintings in the journal feature Meyers himself in the various places that the *Cyane* pulled into port—Valparaiso, Mazatlan, Monterey. He was a ladies' man, never one to miss a party. In most places where he disembarked, he quickly developed a liaison with a local belle and then colorfully bemoaned the cruel fate that separated them and doomed their immortal love the next day as the ship left port. On these pages, Meyers woos and wins "M." in Hawai'i and then bids her farewell in a fit of despondency, as "tears flow." In addition to his large journals, Meyers also wrote letters while onboard, embellishing these too with watercolor drawings. ❖ Three years after his voyage on the *Cyane,* Gunner Meyers was aboard the ship *Dale* when it was dispatched to California to wrest control of Monterey from Mexico. The heavily illustrated diary he kept as a participant in that epic naval contest is in the Roosevelt Library in Washington, DC. His daily musings and drawings together recall momentous historical events from a unique perspective in real time. They reflect a time, place, and personality in ways that traditional history writing cannot.

Honolulu. Oahu

1841

Nov 3. Friday... Stiff breezes. 4 ships outside. inner harbour full. feel an anxious yearning to go on shore. at 12 dinner. at 4 supper. received news that we sail on Monday.

4 Saturday... Strong breezes and a heavy sea on. a Whaleship drag'd to sea at 12 dinner. at 4 Supper brought Enright on board put in irons in the brig. 9 Mutineers from the ship Dartmoor brought on board all ferocious looking villains in the eating line—— one is a youth of about 15 a mere child named Doane

5 Sunday... Stiff breezes. mustered all hands Articles of war read. Service by C. K. Stribling went on shore... found my dear M—— in tears... I now feel really attached to her, after having passed the afternoon with her. had a trying scene— bade de farewell received from her a ring and riband. came on board with a fit of despondency—— tears flow.

6 Monday... Stiff breezes at 8 A.M. Lieut Barry came on board as bearer of despatches for the U.S. got under way. John Laau Wai came on board... bade farewell— standing along the land, watched her hut tile it was no longer visible. then the grove when that was gone, the Mountains. the island untile the distant blue faded altogether. bade—took 9 mutineers out of irons, put them on duty. at 8 reported battery. Some Gentlemen sea sick

7 Tuesday... Stiff breezes head N N E at 12 Lat by Observation 34° 16' N. at 3 Set fore topmast studding sail at 4 Supper at 8 reported

8 Wednesday... Fine weather. after breakfast exercised at general quarters. at 12 dinner Latitude by Observation 26° 56' N... Afternoon broke out the cutlasses employed cleaning them at 8 reported battery. weather very fine—

Waahea Vernau

Robert W. Whitworth

DECEMBER 14, 1846

The country is overgrown with a species of cactus which grows about 20 or 30 feet high and are covered from top to bottom with sharp thorns.

Sixteen-year-old Robert Whitworth's rough-and-tumble diary proves that ignorance is as dynamic—and as much fun—as knowledge. He left Liverpool for adventure and fortune in the United States with no clear plan but carrying a new rifle, which he had purchased in order to "play the deuce with the Buffaloes and Bears." He arrived in New Orleans and decided to go north up the Mississippi for the fare of $2.50. When he lost his rifle and the rest of his luggage to an opportunist thief after customs officials had left his belongings on the dock in disarray, he faced this setback with equanimity and good humor. Penniless, he set out to join the ranks of the American Fur Company trappers and hunters so that he too could spend his earnings once a year in "Riot and Dissipation." He put in a few months on a Missouri farm to buy his passage on a steamboat bound for Fort Leavenworth, and then described the boat's boilers bursting because rosin and pitch had been added to the wood fuel during a race with a second vessel. When he finally arrived safely at his destination, he was "almost immediately seized with a desire to live in one of the little white tents" of the Mormon Battalion of volunteers gathering to fight in the Mexican-American War in the summer of 1846. Whitworth was taken on as a member in short order, qualifying simply by providing his name and date of birth. A soldier more interested in botany than conflict, Whitworth found

prickly brush — these men are
exempt from guard, and carry
nothing but their Tools —
Dec.ʳ 13ᵗʰ Marched 8 miles
Guides came back —
Dec.ʳ 14ᵗʰ Marched 25 miles
to the Settlements of Sonora
Passed a place where the
Sonoranians distill whiskey
from the Muscal Root —
Took too Mexican Soldiers
Prisoners, one of them the
Son of the Governor, of the
town we are now advancing
on — the country here is
hilly barren and prickly
the country is overgrown with
a Species, of Cactus which grow

about 20 or 30 feet high and are
covered from top to bottom with
sharp thorns —

Jonathans or Cactusses
These tall ones we called
Jonathans. being ugly customers
to handle — the other variety
to the right is of frequent
occurrence here. they are both
of a bright green colour

"Candelabra Cactus, Gila Desert,"
C. R. Savage, Views of the great West from
the Missouri River to the Pacific Ocean.

humor in many of the company's grim challenges, such as transporting a team of oxen across a river in wagons at great time and expense, only to see them swim back easily as soon as they reached the other side. What happens to an unsecured floor plank when nails are too dear? What happens when a man from Liverpool tries to emulate the natives and go barefoot in the desert? What is the inevitable fate of a man riding a sweating, recalcitrant, wild mare on a slowly stretching saddle of untanned leather? One day the company was "surprised to see a long line of Indians drawn up across the valley, apparently to give us battle. Our Captain was in high spirits at the prospect of a brush. He rode along our ranks telling us to aim low, aim at the crotch…but [when] it turned out that the Indians did not want to fight, they had just come to pay their respects, we were not sorry, for playing with rifle balls and bows and arrows is a dangerous game. Encamped in a beautiful valley." The diary ends when the company is discharged in Los Angeles on July 16, 1847.

" *Passed a place where the Sonoranians distill whiskey from the Muscal Root—Took two Mexican soldiers prisoners, one of them the son of the governor of the town we are now advancing on—the country here is hilly, barren, and prickly.* **"**

George Hayden

JUNE 19–JUNE 20, 1847

George Hayden filled several small journals that he carried wherever his enlistment in the New York Volunteers took him. Then he copied these worn and stained pages into a single, cleaner volume, sometimes cleaning up the events as well. Joining Stevenson's Seventh Regiment (later known as the First) in New York in September of 1846, he traveled in a three-ship convoy to California to defend US interests in the West during the Mexican-American War. Hayden's diary entries portray a man who may not have enjoyed the military life but welcomed the opportunity to travel and observe new places, plants, animals, and people. He writes unselfconsciously but poetically of the "respiration of the ocean" and the "dry, pure, and elastic air" of the southern San Joaquin Valley; notes the greasy floating mat of krill in the whale fields; and describes three different methods of determining a ship's longitude. Interrupting the sequence of his daily entries are extensive lists in English and Latin of trees, shrubs, grasses, mammals, birds, reptiles, insects, fish, crustaceans, stones, and minerals that he saw upon his way. A truly wide-ranging observer, Hayden describes a near-mutiny aboard ship when the soldiers are required to bathe themselves twice weekly, and notes that volunteers are regularly treated poorly by career soldiers, particularly by Frémont's men. After the regiment reached Monterey and realized that the US was not yet, as they had thought, at war with Mexico, the troops were instructed to load their three-quart India rubber canteens onto freshly mustered horses and travel inland to the Tulare

"Being now on the western plains of the river, we found it very hot in the sun, and the scanty herbage all parched up. Saw many droves of wild horses, some of which contained over 1000. This was a beautiful sight to behold, line after line of these untamed and unfettered steeds were spread out upon the flat plains, as far as the eye could reach, looking in the distance like a large army, drawn out in battle array."

ford here at this almost inaccessible place, at this stage of the river
and we consequently found a large body of water. The horses as usual
were made to swim with nothing but their saddles on, and plunging
at once into deep water, they made their way, landing with much
difficulty about ½ a mile below; we lost only one mule, which was
swept down by the current and lost. Our rafts acted well, most of
the men urging them over by swimming, laying hold of lines attach-
=ed, and all were gotten over in safety. A gloom however, was cast over
the party before we crossed the river, when it was ascertained that
one of the men had been left upon the plains. This young man's
name was Henry Ashton, a native of England and a youth
of much promise. Parties were sent back in every direction, having
to cross the marshes again for the purpose, but no tidings could
they bring of his discovery. Finding it unavailing to stay longer, the
poor fellow was abandoned to his fate, it being the sincere wish and
hope of all that he would either be able to overtake us, or which would be a more prudent course, find his way back again to the Indian
village which we had left on the river above, where, altho they are
wild savages, they may be induced to treat him with kindness.
Before reaching here we killed two Elk, and saw many large hare.
By the long marches of the last few days many of our horses are
completely used up being often without grass, water, or sufficient rest; some we-
=re left behind to shift for themselves, and one or two left dead
on the spot. The spare horses we brought with us proved to be insufficient
for such marches as we make, each man requiring an extra horse.
We had the same difficulties to encounter on the western side
of the river, the marsh being also extensive on that side, though we
had the advantage of daylight in encountering it. All were at
length got through much fatigued and tossed out, and we came to a halt on the
19th ⟩ outside of the slough on the western side on a small affluent
where we rested for a few hours, with but scant provender for the ani-
=mals. Here the Captain preceeded us with his mess making for
the camp of the detatchment forwarded for provisions. This night
we saw many Indian fires and the Coast range was faintly
visible. ✳

June 20th ⟩ Being now on the western plains of the river, we found it very
hot in the Sun, and the scanty herbage all parched up. Saw
many droves of wild horses, some of them containing over 800
steeds, these in running over the plains, raised great clouds of

Lake region on the east side of the Coast Range to subdue horse thieves and Indians accused of "many depredations upon the inhabitants of the plains." Though the Volunteers had a terribly difficult expedition without adequate food and water, building hide boats and tule rafts to cross swollen rivers, Hayden writes that he will "always revert with pleasure to the time of our encampment." He writes of herbal remedies, food plants, and shelters used by the local Indians and describes woven rush drinking cups that were worn by the Indians as hats when not in use, "thus serving in the double capacity of cup and cap." Hayden ends this volume of his diary with an exquisite pencil drawing of a centipede and a wonderful story of a comrade thought lost in the marsh who found his way back to Monterey with the assistance of a grizzly bear.

" *Early this morning we set about building rafts of tulas, each mess of ten men constructing its own raft to convey themselves and luggage over the river, which at this place is pretty wide, but with a current not exceeding four miles an hour, the river in fact being fordable here when in its lowest state.* "

GEORGE HAYDEN AND GEORGE DYER, WATSONVILLE, CALIFORNIA, CA. 1860, BANCROFT PORTRAIT COLLECTION.

Anonymous, New Bedford to San Francisco

JUNE 7–JUNE 8, 1849

> *Boys caught a "molly mock," a black ugly looking bird—in size about that of a turkey. I saw Captain Seaburg throw his iron into a porpoise today from off the martingale under the end of the bowsprit. They are a very handsome formed fish and have a prettily mixed grey and yellowish skin.*

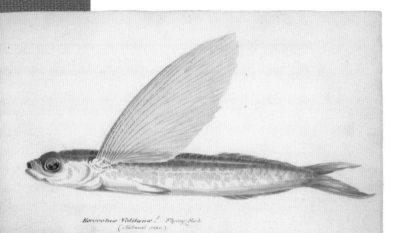

"*Exocetus Volitans*, flying fish, natural size," William Smyth, ca. 1827, Honeyman collection of early Californian and Western American pictorial material.

The keeper of this journal was fascinated by sperm whales, "old settlers," as the captain of his ship called them. When a whale was spotted, he used a kind of stamp technique to note it in his journal—elegant, very cetacean whale depictions—and he listened avidly to the old whalers among the crew, including the captain, who had been on seven whaling voyages. And he never tired of watching the flying fish off the ship's railing. He was a twenty-seven-year-old passenger on the ship *America* out of New Bedford, Massachusetts, bound for the goldfields, "poor, but full of life, health, hope and in pursuit of happiness, on a five-month voyage in quest of gold." Though he had been unfortunate in past pursuits and was unhappy to be separated from his wife and children, he felt confident that this journey would make his fortune. Soon out of Boston, he and several others developed horrible rashes from the dye in their red serge shirts, and so washed them repeatedly in salt water to eradicate the poison. He reports that the passengers were contentious on religious topics and complained when turnips were served for dessert and the water was bad. He quotes conversations and writes wonderfully colorful tales of the travails, rivalries, and arguments, and the particular society aboard ship. He replicates dialects, accents, and figures of speech, and marvels that even a tin pan grows mold in the dampness. His attempts to write in this dampness are frustrated as the pen nib takes up the damp paper finish and creates mush. When the *America* nears San Francisco Bay and very narrowly escapes a collision with rocks hidden by fog, the diarist draws an elaborate diagram of the ship's course as it tacks and navigates to avoid the danger between the Farallones and the Golden Gate.

Journal of a Voyage from New Bedford

Thursday 7 June — This morning the wind is from
the S.W. — continued throughout the night the same
as yesterday — Head a head — Boys caught a "Molly mock"
a black ugly looking bird — in size about that of
a — turkey — I saw captain Seabury throw
his iron into a porpoise to day from off the martin-
gale under the end of bowsprit — They are a very
handsome formed fish and have a prettyly mixed
grey and yellowish skin —

    "These fleetest coursers of the finny race;
    When threatning clouds th'æthereal vault deface,
    Their rout to leeward still sagacious form;
    To shun the fury of th'approaching storm". —

Mr. Macomber "made fast" to a porpoise to day — but lost
him in "getting in" — we had some fine steaks from
the one the Captain killed, for supper — The ballance
was made into sausage meat —

Evening — Wind still from the S.W. "Head a head"
Lat. Ob. 31.44 S. Lon chro. 46.42. W. Bar. 30.00.

to San Francisco Upper California

Friday 8 June — This morning the wind is light
and still from the south — Boys taking over the stern
for birds with porpus blubber — and shooting them with
their rifles — Two porpoises taken to day —

A large 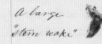 crossed our
"Stern wake"   to day
Acres of porpoises in sight this afternoon — fifty
leaping out of water at one time —
Ship fully trimmed for "rugged weather" —
A new set of sails bent throughout — and rigging
"set up" for the last time this side of "the Horn" —
This Evening we have a continuation of light airs
from the south — as in the morning — Music from the
Glee Club. Lat. Ob. 32,00 S. Lon. chro. 48.06 W. Bar. 30.5/100

I dreamed last night of home! I dreamed my dear
daughter sickened before me, and died! —
I dreamed again — I fancied I was in the midst
of my loved ones! — I opened my arms to receive
and embrace them — but they fell back upon my
breast; and in the excitement of the moment
Exclaimed — If I cannot see you, may Heaven bless
you! — Here the delusion ended; — but I awoke in
me vivid thoughts of those I love, and dreamed about —

"Home! do not mock me, I have none, —   Yet I had once a home I loved;
My native vales are home no more;   I cannot, dare not, say how well;
None kindly for the sternest strand,   Where e'en yet my fondest thought,
Where ocean's wintry billows roar.   My heart's best breathings, lingering dwell.

     I see again the cheering hearth,
     Again each welcome beaming eye;
     I wake, to find how vain the dream,
     And on my lonely pillow sigh."

Isaac W. Baker

AUGUST 16–AUGUST 18, 1849; SEPTEMBER 17–SEPTEMBER 18, 1849

"*Considerable sport with Moses, the tame Crow, who seems remarkably fond of stray pipes, Jack knives, or any other small articles left in his way and who quite familiarly endeavoured to make a third hand at a game of checkers with Goodridge and Dodge.*"

Isaac Baker set out from Boston in 1849 as a working sailor with the forty-strong Beverly Joint Stock San Francisco Company, and in the company of twenty pigs, Kate the dog, Moses the tame crow, who "committed involuntary suicide" by falling overboard six days out, and Katy W. Baker the cat, who inexplicably disappeared five weeks later. Reading his diaries, one develops the notion that Baker was rarely sedentary. A prankster and a man of great curiosity and energy, he had the world at his fingertips—the world he created from the raw material, the nuts and bolts of each twenty-four hours. His pages are filled—"I always write to the bottom of the page, for I like to see the pages well-filled up and for the sake of uniformity"—with puns, doggerel, menus, general mischief, "se(a)rious reflections," tongue-in-cheek "sermons" that include text and "scripture" such as "A little liquor now and then is relished by us sailor men" and "'T'is all for the best." He dubs himself the onboard Town Crier and proclaims, "Fresh

sea sickness however, and what there is, only enough for a specimen —
Morning wind & weather fine, & the company all as lively as — they can
be — considerable sport commencing, and seems to rise with the sun. —
A leetle bit of sickness yet, and a good deal of joking going on. —
Tom — our jolly Tom, very busily at work spoiling the ship's beef
and keeping a sharp look out for prizes. Thinks he saw a cannon
floating by. — Latitude 41° & something over. Longitude 18° 35´.

Acknowledging a draft on Father Neptune! —

Friday Aug 17th — A favorable wind and pleasant weather continued
Every body in good spirits, and enjoying themselves as well as they
can. Two vessels in company which we are fast taking leave
of without ceremony. Considerable sport with MOSES, the
Tame Crow who seems remarkably fond of stray pipes, jack
knives or any other small articles left in his way and who
quite familiarly endeavoured to make a third hand at a
game of checkers with Goodridge and Dodge — Kate
having recovered from sea sickness is busily engaged
washing her face & hands and cleaning her nails. The
Jog having taken possession of the Long boat seems inclined
to dispute the right of search in that vicinity — Latitude
by observation 40° 08´ North.

Saturday, Aug 18th — Light baffling winds, and gradually decreasing
to a calm. From 6 to 8 P.M. the "San Francisco Melodeon Band"
practising a few tunes, and performing for the edification and amuse-
ment of the company. Bass drum, Kettle drum, Cymbals,
Accordeon, Tambourine & Bells in full chorus. Great cry
and some wool. Almost calm — Took in stu'n sails. &

need sharp — throughout the night baffling winds & calms.
Morning squalls from SE with some rain. Almost caught a
shark, but concluded to let him go with a look for his back—
last and our private mark on his back. — Latitude 40° 10´ N.
Sunday Aug 19th — The first Sabbath at sea. the wind "dead ahead"
with squally appearances around. tacked ship took in t gall'n sails
and single reefed the topsails, giving our brand new Sailor men, a
new kink in navigation. Throughout the night more moderate,
but increasing again toward morning, when we double reefed &
kept along quite easily. A ship still in company, and under
snug sail as ourselves. Father Neptune administers another dose
of medicine to his refractory children, much to the distress
of their stomachs. — Some singing & Psalm singing under the
lee of the Long boat. — Impdies around. "Hurrah, hurrah,
"Now then" — "Harpoon, harpoon — "Look at em." O! "Quick"
"get a warp — thats it now. "All ready, and "they're gone
"by Gracious" — Livermore got an unexpected shower bath
by imprudently exposing himself near the "weather fore
rigging" — the "Wonders of Parson Abbott will pray for us to
day — Afternoon (Monday) Wind ahead and squally appearances
all around, weather general expected, and generally obtained too
in this vicinity. — Had an unexpected treat from our Woburn
fiends of a tremendous plump, juicy, nice tomato, which I
enjoyed with a great deal of satisfaction. — Morning, a cross
flobb sea, which knocks the Barque about in a style she's
not been used to. took in a sea over the bow, a part coming
in & deluging the forecastle, and the rest falling back, &
carrying with it our Head board & rail. both sides. making
the Barque look as if her head was shaved for a race! —
"Livermore" with upturned eyes & in piteous accents begs the
man at the helm to "Keep her off or he'd spoil her! then
dodging below exclaims "Isaac, they've carried away all the
braces around the figure head!" — Showers of rain from all
quarters & not much wind. "MOSES (the Crow) got a looking &
missing his foot hold, alighted in the water, but was received
by Dudley, who got as "duck" at the same time. At 12 o'clock
— ship sailed to SW — (No Observation, Sun being obscured

The Forecastle

Is called—the forward part of the ship, the Sailors home, and only castle excepting what he builds in imagination, his parlor, kitchen, dining & sleeping room combined, and his only palace!— Our forecastle, being a little extra, a little larger, and better finished than common; still although calculated to be as comfortable a place as any in them, still it's nothing but a Forecastle, and as such, liable to all the disadvantages of the common lot of such places.— Being in the fore part of the vessel, where of course in stormy weather the spray flies pretty freely on deck, while the water dashes violently against the bows, the Forecastle if not carefully attended to, and often examined outside, is very apt to be wet inside also!— And such has been the case with our "head" quarters of late, and as owing to some very little cause, great trouble ensues, so owing to some little place not properly calked or pitched, or perhaps "shrinking of wood,"—from some cause at any rate, in Wet weather, "when the stormy seas do roll" we are apt to get more than our share of salt water, more than we bargained for, at any rate, and much more uncomfortable than serious, for although the leak or leaks may actually be small as regards quantity of water taken in, still that little scattered about, dripping & dribbling here & there, is something of a nuisance, and also that peculiar unsightly, and unenviable track of Mould that follows afterwards, paying no respect to thing or person.— "Reverse the Engine"! "Bout ship"! and see what we have on this tack,—Ah! Weather fine & nice, thirdsail drawing finely, and throwing good wholesome air into our Forecastle (in exchange for our moist & mouldy climate which soon disappears) our clothing and bedding dry, our chests arranged in good order, our 'deck' (or floor) well scrubbed, swabbed, mopped and swept, and Our Watch below! reading, writing or sleeping, (one or the whole as the case may be,) every body in good spirits, a fair wind to cheer us up, and make us contented, whether or no, because there is a prospect of getting somewhere, then is the time, & here is

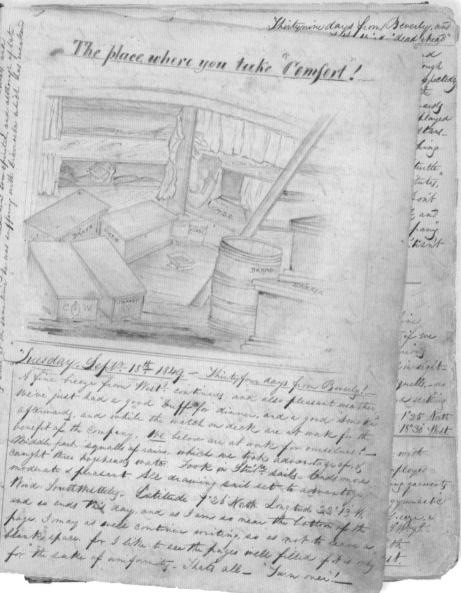

Thirtynine days from Beverly, and

The place where you take "Comfort"!

Tuesday. Sept. 18th 1849.— Thirtyfour days from Beverly!

A fine breeze from West continues, and also pleasant weather. We've just had a good "Duff" for dinner, and a good 'smoke' afterwards, and while the watch on deck are at work for the benefit of the company, We below are at work for ourselves!— Middle part, squalls of rain, which we took advantage of & caught three hogsheads water. Took in Studding sails—took more moderate & pleasant. All drawing sail set to advantage. Wind. South Westerly. Latitude 7°26' North. Longitude 22°13' W. and so ends this day, and as I am so near the bottom of the page, I may as well continue writing so as not to leave a blank space, for I like to see the pages well filled, if it is only for the sake of uniformity. That's all— "Turn over"!—

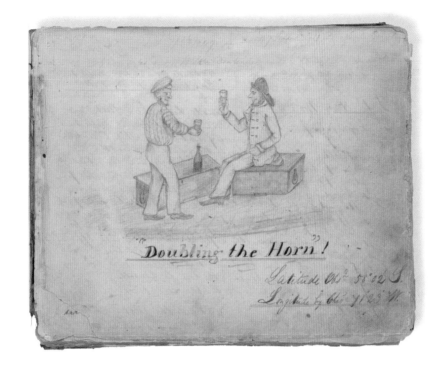

"*Doubling the Horn*"!

Latitude Obs 55°02′ S
Longitude by Obs 71°25′ W

pork once more, once more plum duff. Take hold! Take hold! Sure there's enough. Eat, eat your fill, don't look forlorn. Here's roasted pig and there's Cape Horn, so don't be making such a bother: we'll eat one up and pass the other." He finds fun in the most desperate travail: A smoky house, a scolding wife / Are miseries of the human life. / A leaky ship in squally weather / Is worse than both of these together!" After arriving in Sacramento, Baker tried his hand in the Feather River diggings and marveled that "you can find a sample of all sorts of worlds in California." He gave up the pursuit of gold when his total earnings came out at just forty dollars, leaving California—"that humbug land"—on the bark *Belgrade* a little more than a year after he'd left Beverly.

"The Forecastle, so called, the forward part of the ship: the Sailor's home and only castle (excepting what he builds in imagination), his parlor, kitchen, dining, and sleeping rooms combined, and his only palace."

Jabez D. Hawks

SEPTEMBER 29–OCTOBER 1, 1849

Our dinner today at 3 ½ o'clock consists of a boiled tortilla, a small quantity of mutton and squash. We ordered dinner and they cooked it and ate the largest part themselves. The mountains about here look bare but there are valleys that produce grapes &c where the cattle range.

One seldom hears of the ships that didn't make it to San Francisco during the Gold Rush. J. D. Hawks was a passenger on one of these, the *San Juan*, a small schooner purchased by Hawks and a partner in Panama for twenty-four dollars. It took them forty-nine days to reach Acapulco, each crewmember and passenger suffering "very much for want of provisions and water, being on an allowance of ½ pint of water per day for some three weeks…" Fifty-one days later, and still off the coast of Mexico, Hawks and nine other passengers left the ship to continue north on land. Abandoned by their guide, their mule stolen, their horses dead of dehydration, the party resorted to foraging for mussels and wild plants and drinking salty water from holes they dug. Hawks's daily entries nevertheless include account records, language translations, and lists of provisions, as well as drawings of the towns and churches that they passed on their arduous way. Along with the physical appearance of a diary—the color of its paper and the wear of its cover—drawings bring other senses into the mix; one can smell the dog and feel the heat of midday. The whole group finally and safely reached San Diego, where they boarded a northbound ship and arrived in San Francisco on October 10, 1849. At long last the ill-fated *San Juan* reached San Francisco, too—but not until the latter part of December. Hawks became a life member of the Society of California Pioneers until his death in San Francisco, twenty years after his arrival.

Courtesy of the Society of California Pioneers, San Francisco, California.

56

hut where they were slaughting a Beef
& where we bought some "pinoles" a small
nut found in the mountains – They represent
the Indians about here as being very bad
We found a Spaniard at the Mission from whom
we bot some Eggs & cheese & had a few tortillas
made – We pass several Oaks or species of the
Quercus which bear acorns – The small shrubs
like the bush of the Current or Gooseberry are
full of acorns half grown – The leaf of these
trees are not shaped like the Red oak of our
Country but the leaf is small like the Peach or
Plum – At 7½ o'clock we arrived at the
old Mission of El Descanso Soon after
arriving we boiled a pot of Corn & ate it for supper
We also purchased a half of a sheep & we
also boiled that for breakfast tomorrow

   Sunday ~~Friday~~ Sept 30 1849
"El Descanso"
   Our mules are in such a condition that our
Contractor & guide says he can go no farther to
-day & we shall be obliged to remain here till
tomorrow morning – ~~This is very annoying as we
are so near to San Diego & it is important we should
get there as soon as possible~~ This old Mission
is like all the others we have passed in Ought
-lines – The Church is occupied as a sheep pen
& a family live in a part of the rest of the
building which has a roof – several Indians are
living in the valley & there is a Tribe of savages
about 4 leagues from here – They are very bad
& troublesome – It is strange how these people

59

live – I saw some eating the Corn stalks to day
they Eat any & Every thing they can get –

El Descanso

Our dinner to day at 3½ o'clock consists of
a boiled Tortilla a small quantity of mutton & squash
We order dinner & they cooked it & ate the largest part
themselves – The mountains about here look bare
but there are vallies that produce grass &c where
the Cattle range –

   Monday Oct 1st 1849

We left El Descanso at 9 o'clock
& traveled over a very good road for
4½ or 5 leagues to an Indian Rancho where
He has figs. Corn. Melons. &c It is a pretty
little valley – We encamped at dark in
small valley without water – I saw a
fine herd of Deer to day, there were about
30 – We also saw a fine lot of seal on the
rocks –

Anonymous, Boston to San Francisco

NOVEMBER 30–DECEMBER 1, 1849

> *Last night we enjoyed the queen of full moons. She was all night bright, brilliant and beautiful, peerless to behold. I was awake as I always am at the different watches in the night and looked out of my little window upon the still silent beauty of the night and naught could I hear save the tramp of the night watch upon the quarterdeck. The gale had abated and all was hushed in infant stillness and repose.*

When time seems to fly by, keeping a journal can both slow and mark it. Paradoxically, many sea travelers have sought solace and occupation in pen and page during the slow burdensome passage of shipboard time. The act of drawing requires other attentions as well, and so adds to the hours fulfilled. Though the keeper of the log of the brig *Wellingsley* in 1849 is unknown, his personality is revealed in this intensely personal record. Each entry is addressed to "My Dear Wife," and homesickness for Gussy and their daughter, Annie, is pervasive. At the end of the first of two twin books, he writes, "Here ends the first volume of my journal, which I hope may afford you as many hours of pleasure to read as it has your husband to write—twelve long weeks ago this very afternoon since we reluctantly parted." His father-in-law was also onboard and occupied the bunk below, though he was "on deck at most all hours of the night like a good and faithful sentinel, always on the watch tower." ❖ To maintain his page-per-day format, the anonymous journal keeper sometimes used cross writing, inscribing the page at a ninety-degree angle over the previous entry. In an ornate copperplate hand in sepia ink on blue tinted paper, the author describes the weather and shipboard activities—including his attempt to make tapioca pudding without eggs or milk—and draws the

Friday November 30th (89 Days)

Last night we enjoyed the queen of Fall moons. She ran all night bright, brilliant and beautiful, peerless to behold. Long smooth as glass, and at the different watches in the night, and looking out of my little window upon the still silent beauty of the night and naught could I hear save the tramp of the nightly watch upon the quarter deck. The Gale had abated and all was hushed in silent stillness and repose. We sat up in the Cabin reading and talking until near two. We felt a strong disposition to play whist, but could not as we need minus the cards. So I went to bed and lay and think of my Darling Wife & Children, and wondered how you would all pass the Evening at home. Could I have given mines of Gold, did I possess them, could I have been with you. Oh how much I thought of you all and our old New England home. Soft day! We have all been busy at work. The Day has been lovely. We have had almost a head wind since the Gale left us which we consider rather hard treatment. To Day we captured a large wild Sea Hen which fluttered about, and squeaked out anything but agreeable music and protested against being made a prisoner. It was no use to contend with Mr H. for in few moments he gave it to the Mist for a Thanksgiving Dinner & &c. So Ended that awful tragedy. Sam Thatcher has had his whole wardrobe on Deck all day and truly adventures all together making quite a clothes household display. Shirts were offered at five Dollars each. No purchasers, for want of funds. We have not seen a vessel for a long time. We should like to for Company's Sake. Our Sick men have recovered and all ate their good Thanksgiving Dinner yesterday with great gusto. We have continued the Celebration of the day by another Leg of Pork Roasted to day and served by our Steward. — In Truth — you would not for a moment doubt that we had an Extraordinary Dinner. Sam Thatcher contributed much to our happiness yesterday by his Stories, Jokes, Fun &c.

Saturday December 1st (90 Days)

Dear Wife This is the first day of rough storm and icy winter at Home, and the first day of Sweet June with us, and consequently the beginning of lovely Summer Months off Cape Horn. So far as that is concerned it is truly delightful to contemplate the future season which will make the residue of our voyage very pleasant. We have nothing to dread nor murmur at but head winds, gales & calms & Fair Sailing of which we have already been favoured with. This has been a lovely Sweet Scented Summer day. We have had all the full beauty and force of the Sun since the morning and it still sends its rays into our Cabin where I am now writing, and we have been to Tea, and it is after 7 — 5 at Home with you, and dark more than an hour ago, you are all seated round your Tea Table by Star light. And I can picture sweet Anna by her dear Mother's side busy trying to help herself to her dear Grandma's goodies which do abound at this season of the year. You know how much I should a Saturday night. Spend at home. Consequently my heart and its strong desires are with you all now. Here I should love to step in and see you, On deck this morning at 3. For the purpose of seeing the round full shining moon and a fine fair wind all of which was well fitting. Up to see the Stars too was beautiful. I have been engaged all day in exposing my wardrobe on deck to the fine wind and pure air. My stock of Boots and Shoes also I found them all in a state of mould and moth and made me a good smart days work to clean the same which I hope will be beneficial to them, as I needed to the tune of a touch of the Rheumatism and tooth ache. But, nothing serious. I have just been called on deck to witness a clear and brilliant Sun set. She dipped into old Neptune precisely at 16 minutes after Seven. Sam Thatcher is on deck telling Stories Full of Fun and anecdote.

A view of the Land as seen on the Coast of California, on board Brig Willingsly.

May 2d, 3d, and 4th, 1850.

10 Miles Distant.

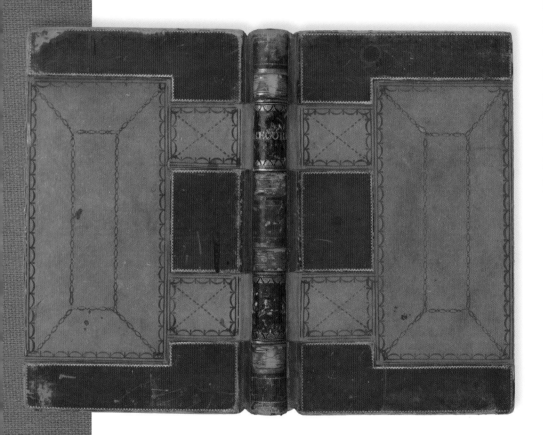

coasts of Cape Horn, Chile, and Tierra del Fuego over the railing of the ship as he passes them by. "Amidst the homesickness and weariness of sea life, I have felt a touch of sublimity, and could for hours stay on deck and admire the dark wild roaring waters of Old Ocean." The sorrowful poetry he inscribes on the pages is as elegant and ornate as his cursive script. Regrettably for us, the log ends after the brig arrives in San Francisco in May 1850, as many Gold Rush diaries did. We're left to wonder if Gussy and Annie in Boston ever saw it.

> " *We sat up in the cabin reading and talking until near ten. We felt a strong disposition to play whist but could not as we were minus the cards so I went to bed and lay and think of my Darling Wife & Child, and wondered how you would all pass the evening at home. I would have given mines of gold did I possess them could I have been with you.* "

Nelson Kingsley

JANUARY 22–JANUARY 26, 1850

"I find there is nothing like trying." Nelson Kingsley began his diary
when he left his native Connecticut and continued writing throughout
his two years in the diggings and until he boarded a ship outbound
from San Francisco in March 1851. Though engaged to Miss E. W. and
acknowledging it "a great and hazardous undertaking for a green Yankey,"
ingenious woodworker and musician Kingsley joined a group of joint
stock holders on the bark *Anna Reynolds*. Prior to sailing he worked with
his partners to prepare the ship, which would carry a deck-top cabin they
called "The Senate" and the materials for a steamboat to take the group
up the Sacramento River and provide shelter in the goldfields. While
at sea, the men made tents, mining equipment, and the fixtures for the
steamboat, struggled with washing dishes in ice-slushy saltwater, and had
nightly debate meetings, entertaining such topics as whether or not early
marriage is conducive to happiness, whether the greater influence on
men is wealth or women, if capital punishment is a deterrent to crime,
and "was the manner in which our forefathers treated the Aboriginees
justifiable, and after considerable able argument on both sides was decided
in the negative." Kingsley also carved a flute "verry perfect in tone,"
tried to master the braiding of grass hats, and formed a society "for the
improvement of reading." When the ship made a stop, Kingsley would
dispense books and tune pianos for the locals, but blasted the selfish agents

> *Many are the wishes & wants of those who
> are so unfortunate as to be sick in this country,
> no good bed, no experienced physician, no
> dainties to touch a delicate appetite, and so
> far from home & friends makes many of them
> worse in their disease than they would be with
> a free mind, and kind friends to soothe the
> pillow of affliction.*

Jan 20th 1850

22nd tue Pleasant and warm to day with a light breeze from the south, Worked on the Steamboat, put the streaks on her sides, but have used up the nails and shall have to wait until we can send for some, we got on about half of the side, the sick about the same

23rd wed A cloudy day and some rain, with a strong S E wind towards night, worked at hewing some sticks for horses to use the Pit-Saw, as this may with some labor pay well to saw some of the oaks that stand near us into stuff suitable to use about the boat. Five started for San Francisco for nails and other articles

24th thurs Rained all day, and a strong wind this morning from the S.E it has rained uncommon hard until just at night whent it partly cleared away but soon blew and rained again went into the Hospital to take care of the sick with Mr Eatons, it is a task for two persons to do it as there is five to attend to

January   103   1851

and sometimes there is many things to be done at the same time No money would hire me to go in and stay but duty compels, and necessity calls it, that all must be done to assist nature that can be to save life Many are the wishes & wants of those who are so unfortunate as to be sick in this country, no good bed no experienced physician, no dainties to touch a delicate appetite, and so far from home & friends makes many of them worse in their disease than they would be with a free mind, and kind friends to sooth the pillow of affliction But such is life and vain is the help of man when God so wills it, So it renders it the best way for us to wade through the mire of misfortune to gain a "better land" in days to come, and seek to do the will of an allpowerful Creator & Preserver that we may gain an eternal rest in the kingdom prepared for those that love and serve him

25 fri. Cloudy with but little rain, worked at fixing the Pit-Saw. but little interest in the camp to day as far as work is concerned, as no man is or seems to have any interest in thing as far as work is concerned, I hope that different time will appear before long or all must stop

26th sat Some rain to day weather comfortably warm which is & has along back No extremeties of heat & cold as in the Eastern states A boat came down the river with four men in it going on a hunting excursion one of which had been in the mines on the Yuba, He gave flattering accounts of the gold in that

for their cheating travel arrangements, "All talk and no cider." He wrote that drawing likenesses "tell to mind volumes at a glance." After many delays and after briefly considering going into the lumber business instead of mining, the group successfully reached their goal in the northern mines, setting up the small deck cabin on land as a hospital. They were modestly successful in their profits, and Kingsley was emboldened to overwinter a second year and keep working the streambed with their ship-made equipment, but he quit the claim in February of 1851 and sailed home the following month. He wed Miss E. W. upon his return but died soon after, in 1852. ❧ The legend next to the drawing in his journal reads, "A California Stew. As we journey through life there is many incidents as they transpire are interesting & sometimes deeply so, one of these took place to day. In the picture are myself & my friend Eaton back from the camp some 200 rods to which place we have been nearly over our boots in water to get to, and are privately enjoying ourselves over a dish of *molasses candy*. The one sitting nearest represents myself and the one stirring molasses Mr. E at the same time talking of home & Dear Friends."

"SACRAMENTO CITY," CA. 1850, HONEYMAN COLLECTION OF EARLY CALIFORNIAN AND WESTERN AMERICAN PICTORIAL MATERIAL.

Isaac Sherwood Halsey

MARCH 14–MARCH 15, 1850

Polished drawings of ships are a common addition to many nineteenth-century diaries. Often the drawing is on the frontispiece or endpaper of the diary and is the only illustration present in the volume. Frequently the draftsman appears not to have been the diarist. I imagine a sailor skilled with a pen who offered of an evening to draw a portrait of their vessel in the journals of passengers. But Isaac Halsey was the artist as well as the writer of this diary recounting his voyage at age twenty on the ship *Salem*, which set sail from New York to San Francisco in 1849. With his brother, uncle, and one hundred and fifty other members of the California Mutual Benefit Association of New York, Halsey purchased and outfitted the ship and spent seven months sailing down the coast of South America, around Cape Horn, and north to California, having succumbed to the "yellow fever" which caused them to leave "peaceful and valuable homes" to dig for gold. "Thank fortune," there were also "Seven Ladies on board to throw around our dreary position a few rays of Sunshine." Halsey subsequently worked as a miner in American Camp, Murphy's Diggings, Mokelumne Hill, and Volcano, and as a storekeeper, a stereographic photographer, and finally as a dentist in Oakland. ❧ The original diary is frayed, brittle, and coverless and is missing the pages bearing the entries between March 13 and October 10, but at some point Halsey began the task of copying the diary into another volume. Shown is the recopied version with entries for the third and fourth day of the voyage, when Halsey fears he must "suspend writing till I get well, for this Sea Sickness is, oh! so hororable." By March 17 he is feeling well enough to enjoy the "ladies singing sacred music on the promenade deck" and to do "the whole routine of Housewifery—making beds, washing, mending, etc." He writes dolefully, "What a blessing a good wife would be now!"

> "*When I came on deck this morning I found myself for the first time in my life out of sight of land, and nothing to rest the eye upon but the mighty waters around us, the wet clouds above us, an occasional sea gull flying to and fro, and our own floating island.*"

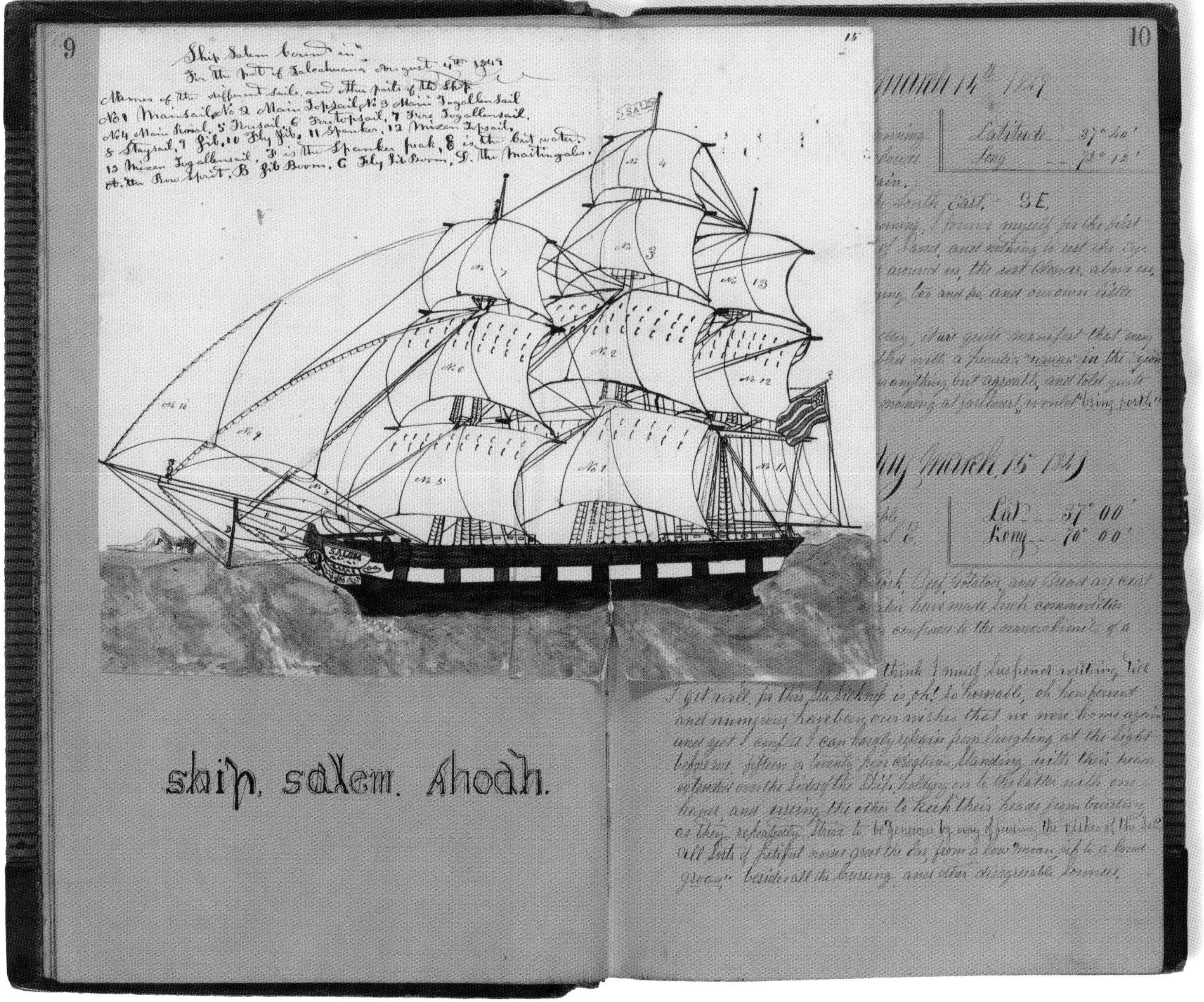
9
10
Ship Salem bound in
For the Port of Talcahuana August 4th 1849
Names of the different sails and other parts of the Ship
No 1 Mainsail, No 2 Main Topsail, No 3 Main Topgallantsail
No 4 Main Royal, 5 Foresail, 6 Foretopsail, 7 Fore Topgallantsail,
8 Staysail, 9 Jib, 10 Fly Jib, 11 Spanker, 12 Mizen Topsail,
13 Mizen Topgallantsail, F is the Spanker peak, E is the Cut water,
A the Bow Sprit, B Jib Boom, C Fly Jib Boom, D the Maitingals.
SALEM
Latitude 37° 40'
Long 72° 12'
Lat 37° 00'
Long 70° 00'
skip, salem. rhoda.

Thomas Kerr

MAY 27–MAY 28, 1850

Misfortune and despair haunt every page of Thomas Kerr's journal. Fleeing the Irish potato blight, disease, and famine of 1849, he impulsively left his new wife and son in Londonderry on his twenty-fourth birthday to enter the California gold lottery. He arrived in California but never mined a grain of gold. An arduous, wearisome voyage with poor rations was followed by illness and poverty in San Francisco, where he languished, lacking funds enough to get to the goldfields. With his training as a draftsman, he finally hired on as a builder but lost his stake repeatedly in bad deals, supply delays, fires, and any number of instances of rotten luck. En route to a job building an "iron house" near Marysville, the schooner he rode in was becalmed, so Kerr and his mates spent a week blistering their hands, pulling the boat against the current with ropes tied to stumps alongside the Sacramento River, "this Cursed Slough," engulfed in clouds of tormenting "muskeatoes." His sole pleasures were watching the small purple hummingbirds and playing his trumpet-like cornopean. He wrote in anguish on June 8, 1850, that his mind was in a very bad state. "I have truly regretted coming to Calafornia, Yes and even I went farther, sorry that I ever were born to such a world of trouble." He resorted to selling his socks and handkerchiefs in order to eat, but two years later was able to

"MARYSVILLE, YUBA COUNTY, CALIFORNIA," HONEYMAN
COLLECTION OF EARLY CALIFORNIAN AND WESTERN
AMERICAN PICTORIAL MATERIAL.

102

7th Monday 27th May 1850 Towards Eliza City.

Had been very much annoyed last night and thro' the day
by those dreadful pests of Musketoes. the Cabin is
Crammed Chalk full when at Breakfast had to run.
on deck with my bowl of Coffee and piece of Bread. and
at Dinner had to run on deck also with my plate and
there finish Dinner. between those and the exposure to
a Burning Sun I must say we are miserable. for only
knows how long we may be thus situated. there is not the
slightest appearance of wind. the Capt curses at a great
rate, and being a Yankee he ushers out some new Coined
ones too. his expenses are he tells me 30 dollars p day.

At half past 6 P.M. we got under Sail and I think
we shall be out of this Cursed Slough. and get rid of the pests
of Blood thirsty vagabonds. that take Such delight in
extracting the last drops if possible. Sometime before
we Sailed Mills and I got the boat and Sailed to the upper
Site Side of river where 3 or 4 Yankees have settled
down to market Garden. we did not think much of
what experience they show in Gardening. but I like
to see agriculture get into the Country even upon
a Small scale. the man we addressed seemed a respec
=table and intelligent person he had peas fit for
table asked 4 dollars p lb for them. the turnips were
a promising crop but had them much too close
potatoes looked well but planted them rather queer
in clusters about 2 yards square. he had been
mowing down weeds. the ground he intends preparing
for potatoes. he says it aint too late for them yet.
they chaps has nearly half an acre under Crop.
Indian corn he has to the height of 3 or 4 feet.
and is also a vinery plantation which Seems to look well
but seems young. vines grow most Luxuriant with here
along the Banks of the river and will probably be
Grapes. but p not hitting on another month. after 5 hours
pretty good Sailing the wind slacks. so we came to an anchor for the
night

103

8th Tuesday 28th May 1850
Towards Eliza City. River Sacramento

Slept very well last night had not been at all annoyed by the
Musketoes. the night being rather cold they kept in the Cabin.
Got up at 4 oc and in half an hour after we were on our way.
Sacramento City being 25 miles off. as we get along. I see
many settlers squatting down by the side of the river and
doing more a less at farming the following is a Diagram of
one in particular that took my eye. being made of Canvass.

It will be observed that one
window has got a shash and
glass in the other has neither.
there are many rustic cottages
by the banks. and at each
house will generally be seen an empty barrel or two. the river
widens a little but not to the width of the River Tople. from about
half past 10 till half past 12 oc we had another twist of Warping
or dragging along by the rope. and there in the calm 5 or 6 vessels
were lying. however we all managed to under Sail again. we
passed here. a Barque called the Ocean Bird she passed us 4
days ago in the Slough. about 5 oc we passed a small village by the
side of the Sacramento river called Suttersville being only 2 miles from Sacra

city. and at 7 oc we got into the latter we went ashore for an hour.
About 9 oc we were under sail again. Young McSwain and his friend
were nearly left behind as ar. as they did not meet the Capt at the
time he appointed we shouts. to go aboard so after waiting for them
½ an hour. we started up to the schooner that lay some 80 yards and in
the river. when I got aboard I took my Cornopean thinking they might
it which they did. and Called on us. One of the sailors & I went for
them in the Boat. at this time the vessel was under sail & the Anchor
ready up. before we could overtake them again they were nearly
a mile out of town. they had to lie too or we would not catch them

"SIERRA BUTTES MINE BRASS BAND,"
OLIVER FAMILY PHOTOGRAPH COLLECTIONS.

"Had been very much annoyed last night and thro' the day by those dreadful pests of muskeatoes: the cabin is crammed chalk full, when at breakfast had to run on deck with my bowl of coffee and piece of bread, and at dinner had to run on deck also with my plate and then finish dinner, between those and the exposure to a burning sun I must say we are miserable. God only knows how long we may be thus situated, there is not the slightest appearance of wind: the Capt curses at a great rate, and being a Yankee he ushers out some new coined ones too."

send for his wife, Elizabeth, and son, James, to join him, supporting them with work as a bookkeeper and as a salesman for a wholesale grocer, and living in California until his death in 1888. In 1849 he titled his journal "DIARY OF THINGS WORTH NOTICE—DURING MY VOYAGE TO CALAFORNIA—& REMARKABLE EVENTS THERE." A year and half later, he added a subtitle, "Yes and a good many things not worth notice too."

J. L. Akerman

JUNE 28–JULY 4, 1850

When J. L. Akerman arrived in San Francisco on the *Daniel Webster* from Boston in April of 1850, he was not impressed by the charms of the city, finding it so dull that he boarded a schooner for Sacramento just four days after his arrival. After stocking up on supplies there, he and his partners struck out for Salmon Falls on the Yuba River, setting up camp near Downieville. He not only wrote about his own travails in "digging all day," but noted the political and social situations around him. Though admonished by the tax collector to report "foreigners"—including California Indians—who hadn't paid their twenty dollars per month to dig, Akerman decided to turn a blind eye. When he felt so ill from "a pain in his side" that he determined to take a day off and make a bush bed on which to rest, he instead climbed a peak simply because he had long had the desire but not the leisure to do so. From the summit, he reveled in the "glorious view" of the Sacramento Valley, the Coast Range, and the Sierra Nevada. ❖ Popular letter-sheet stationery imprinted with western scenes and sold to lonely miners to write home on may have inspired hand-illustrated diaries like Akerman's. He went on to travel widely throughout California, visiting and describing different mining communities, but he was particularly partial to theater. He later worked as a prompter and scenery painter in San Francisco, Grass Valley, and Nevada City before his return to the East Coast in 1857.

> *We met on our way a Chinese that was bound up to Georgetown in search of his brother who had just come into the country. He appeared a very intelligent fellow, could talk very good English. He has a company of forty Chinamen up on the Yuba to work for him. He paid their passage out from China and they are to work for him at four dollars per day for five months.*

Falls a large number have come in to day one came in
with three squaws two of them were quite good looking girls the
best that I have seen they sat down on the bank near our tent
I went out and sat down with them gave them some bread
for which they were thankful one of them took me by the hand
and made signes for me to go into house with her but I
declined I let her lead me as far as the Lymn tent there
I stopt and she went back to the others many of the Indians
have been into our tent to day some of them will catch a salmon
at the falls carry him over to town and sell him and get
a bottle of rum on their way back they will stop at our
tent to get water and have a drink all round some of them
are quite drunk to day one of them stole a large fish
to day and was running over to town to sell it when
some of them gave chase to him they caught them him
just below our tent but he would not give up the fish
so they had a reguar set to but they did not display much
sense in fighting It has been very hot to day
at night I loaded my pistol and put it at the head
of my berth did not know but that the Indians would
be round in the night

July 1st Not feeling hardly able to go to work
To day Bell and I have been on a prospecting
tour we have been out about six miles into a
ravine where we heard there was good diggins
we found there four men to work who were

from four to six Dollars a day on an average some
days they would not make hardly anything then they
would strike a small place that would pay very
well one man found a piece a few days before we
were there that weighed $23 we met on our
way a chinese that was bound up to george town in
search of his Brother who had just come into the country he appeared to a very inteligent fellow could
talk very good english he has a company of forty
Chinamen up on the Yuba to work for him he paid
their passage out from china and they are to work
for him at four dollars per day for five months he
said that he had been on to the Feather river into
the mountains and prospected where he got one dollar to
a pan out of top dirt says the Bars there are
very rich we found a rifle which we brought
home arrived home about 4 in the afternoon kept
a trail all the way from the ravine home

4th To day is the Aniversary of our National Inde-
pendence we got up this morning a little after 12 oclock
and fired a salute heard them firing over in town
loaded up our guns and pistols and started over on
our way over we thought we would give Merrill a salute
as we were going by his tent but before we got quite
to the tent the philosipher saw us and thought that
we were Indians he rushed into the tent to alarm
the rest but before he got them awake we let slip
and such a hullabaloo as they made the poor fellows
scared most to death they rushed out of the tent
in all directions we went over in town
and saluted packwood and marm freeseyourleg
came home and turned in fired another salute
in the morning another at noon and at sundown
in the evening they had a Ball at Plumbs Hotel four
ladies present

Isaac W. Baker

JULY 23–JULY 25, 1852; AUGUST 22, 1852

On his second voyage to the West Coast, in 1852, Isaac Baker again worked as a member of the crew and entertained the passengers between watches, distracting the ladies from their seasickness by "taking them to the beach on the best horses" (barrels on deck), by staging plays about King Neptune and his wife, On Amplify, and by recruiting members for the San Francisco Melodeon Band. Still, it is the pigs for which he reserves his most picturesque and incorrigible playfulness. As each is slaughtered to augment the monotonous Sunday rations, Baker embellishes his journal pages with verses and drawings of the event and anticipates with relish the coming feast of "sea pie," a mariners' layered meat pie. ❧ This trip, Baker remained in California long enough to learn the daguerreotype trade and drove a mobile studio wagon around the mining camps before returning to Massachusetts in 1853, where he hired himself out to deliver lectures based on the eyewitness sketches in his diaries, complete with hand-painted life-sized backdrops. He may have gone to Australia in search of gold, and he may have died in Sumatra in 1862, but the story of this playful and restless adventurer is obscure after his second journal ends. Wherever Baker was, he was completely in the moment, a wacky incarnation of the adage "the journey is the destination."

ISAAC BAKER AND FRIEND, PHOTOGRAPH BY ISAAC BAKER.
COLLECTION OF THE OAKLAND MUSEUM OF CALIFORNIA,
GIFT OF THE ART GUILD.

Seventy-six days from Boston
for San Francisco

Friday July 23ᵈ 1852

Continual squalls of hail & rain
from N to N. turned out & took in reefs. set and made
sail to accommodate them. "Cold work, I tell you!"
sails wet.—(Cotton sails aint stiff when they're wet!
O no!—) reef points stiff—fingers numb,—hail stones
sharp, and rather cutting. (especially on any one
blessed with such a proboscis as mine.) and on
the whole, rather interesting times for the month of
July, but then we are in   Latitude 40°45 South
                                 Longitude 56°58 W

Saturday July 24th

A couple furious hail squalls
to commence this day, towards night more pleasant
and finally clear weather through the night Wind
Northwesterly & the double reefs turned from topsails. top
gallant sails set. &c—   Latitude 41°55 S
                              Longitude 57°12 W

Sunday July 25th

Northwest winds & a heavy swell from
S.W. weather pleasant & moderate breezes inclining to
S.W. towards morning. Latter part the same.
Lady passengers muster strong on deck once more
All sail set once more.   Latitude   43°23 South
                          Longitude 58°29 West

Ode to my old stocking!

Heelless and toeless work of art
Alas! thou't getting old,
So worn and torn I scarcely know
The relict I behold!—

Thy foot, sore scratch'd by many a nail
In many a place worn thin,
Indeed 'twould be a darned hard task
To make you whole again!—

Reef points stiff, fingers numb, hail stones sharp, and rather cutting (especially on any one blessed with such a proboscis as mine) and on the whole, rather interesting times for the month of July.

Goat Island and *Northwest extremity of*
Juan Fernandez

Sunday. August 22d 1852   106 days from Boston.
Fine Westerly winds &
passing Clouds. At daylight the Island of Juan
Fernandez in sight. centre bearing N½E. by
Compass. distant about thirty-five miles—
Stood in for the Island. hove to, & sent boat ashore
with six water casks. "filled away" and "stood
off & on" waiting their return. and so ends this
day (sea account) in Latitude 33° 45 South
Longitude 78° 59 West,

or thereabouts, being "lying off and on" near the
village of Cumberland; Island of Juan Fernandez

Poor Bess is dead, and Jockey mourns
Her loss, but all in vain,—
The Cook, his task perform'd too well
She'll never breathe again.—

And nevermore within yon pen,
With upturned glance so sly,
And that good natur'd grunt will she
Salute each passer by!

No more shall "Swill" with scouse, or mush,
Your hungry stomach feed,—
Alas. for all these dainties now
Sweet Bess thou hast no need.

Cheer up young Jockey. dry your tears,
For just as like as not,
You soon will follow after Bess,
And she has gone to—Pot!

Farewell sweet Bess. thy loss I mourn,
My garments sure I'll rend—
My story's finish'd. tail out short
And here you see the

End

> *Cheer up young Jackey, dry your tears,*
> *or just as like as not,*
> *You soon will follow after Bess,*
> *And she has gone to…Pot!*

Robert Eccleston

AUGUST 10–AUGUST 18, 1853

Robert and his younger brother Richard Eccleston both kept beautifully illustrated diaries during their travels and sojourns in California. Robert began to make entries in his first journal in 1849, when he set out at age twenty-one with the Fremont Association of New York in the company of another brother, Edward. Most of the fractious group gave up the journey when they finally reached Galveston, Texas, discouraged by erroneous directions, Indian wars, cholera, poverty, and the unnerving prospect of some two thousand miles of wilderness yet to be crossed, but the brothers persevered. Ultimately dissatisfied with the results of their mining efforts, Robert dug out enough to stake another overland journey to purchase a herd of sheep in Missouri and return with them to California and take up ranching near Marysville. ❧ Though the prose in this journal is sparse, his precise drawings elegantly compensate for any omission. A subsequent diary covers his tenure with Major James Savage and Corporal Kirkpatrick when the Mariposa Battalion chanced upon Yosemite Valley while pursuing Indians in the Sierra Nevada. He titled an 1855 journal "Life at Garden Ranch." The diaries show a man resolutely elbowing out a place for himself among the Indians, Californios, and cattle rustlers. He had a particular fondness for drawing horses and mules. The week before the page shown here, Eccleston had traveled to Chico to watch a horse race at Bidwell's Ranch with a ten-thousand-dollar purse. The days following this entry were spent driving his horses home from "the best range in California" and trying to track down a missing mule.

ROBERT ECCLESTON,
BANCROFT PORTRAIT COLLECTION.

> *The horse greatly disappointed his friends, who came to the conclusion he was no race animal and the stallion of fine blood valued at $10,000 came down to a low figure in the estimation of those who witnessed his effort. The day was warm and melons and refreshments flew fast. The distance run ½ mile.*

One of his illustrations depicts a Californian treed by a grizzly bear and includes a note by Eccleston that he had originally intended the drawing to illustrate Edward Young's long poem "Night Thoughts; On Life, Death, and Immortality." ❖ Before his death at eighty-one, Eccleston implored his children and grandchildren to help him transcribe the twelve diaries, either for publication or for posterity, but only one was ever completed, *The Mariposa Indian War, 1850–1851.*

"VAQUERO"

A Lass Horse.

Andrew Jackson Grayson

SEPTEMBER 19–SEPTEMBER 28, 1853

Sickly as a child, Andrew Grayson spent hours watching and drawing wildlife in his native Louisiana. When his teacher caught him drawing birds in class, Grayson was removed from school by his father and sent to business college in Missouri, forbidden to draw. Later, while in commerce, he would roam the woods, leaving his clerk to mind the store. When the business failed, he resolved to move west in 1846 with his new wife, Frances Timmons, and their son, Edward, traveling part of the way with the unfortunate Donner Party. In 1853, while living in San Jose and after seeing an exhibit of Audubon's birds, Frances encouraged Andrew to begin painting again. He taught himself paint mixing and taxidermy and began traveling in order to compile his now-celebrated *Birds of the Pacific Slope*, which remained unpublished during his lifetime. ❖ When he wrote this "little journal" in 1858, Grayson was feeling corpulent and out of shape, unable to hunt successfully. Running into an old acquaintance, Von Schmidt, on the street in San Francisco, he impulsively signed on to accompany a surveying trip down the San Joaquin Valley. He wrote that he wanted to go because he hadn't yet been to the Tulare region but had often heard of the great abundance of wildlife there. So he went to San Jose to take back his tried and true friend, a Dickson rifle, from the person who'd borrowed it and bid farewell to his wife. ("I hope my son will take care of her when I am no more, but I hope no one will get her who does not know how to use her—and use her well.") During the three-month

> *"Came across a herd of antelope but they were so wild I could not get near enough to shoot one, not without creeping a long way over a hot and barren plain. My corpulancy and the hot weather would not justify me in doing this."*

A few miles after we had crossed the river, we saw a large track of a Grisley which seemed to have just crossed the road. We soon made preparations to follow his trail, for Von is always ready for a hunt. After tracking him through the woods for a while, I came to the conclusion that the old Growler had made tracks to the river to quench his thirst & cool his hide — for the day was melting hot, and the hills around parched. I could not conceive what brought him so far from water at that time of day, and such a day! —

We encamped upon "dry Creek" this evening a hole of bad water we found here — after getting some hay and barley from a house situated here and partaking of our supper we laid down to sleep — but the flies were bad, and the moon shining in our faces prevented me from resting very well —

Sept 20th By Sun rise we were on the road — crossed the Tuolumne river at Dickersons ferry Mr Dickerson is an old acquaintance, having crossed the plains with his family when I did in /46 — he showed me a pumpkin which he said he raised measuring Six feet and one inch in circumferance!! — which I considered some pumpkins

the Surveyor General —

Sept 28th Von here commenced his work, which was to make a correction of the line he ran last season, as far as the four creeks — This error was made Von says by the great variation of the compass — he will now run with a transit by takeing a polar observation every night — —

I went out hunting in the low hills for Antilope, but found none, then came down on the plaines again far ahead of the waggons, and came across a herd of antilope but they were so wild I could not get near enough to shoot one, not without creeping a long way over a hot and barren plaine, my corpulancy and the hot weather would not justefy me in doeing this.

As I started to return I saw two men comeing across the plaines towards me we both regarded each other suspeciously — but on comeing up found it to be Mr Tracy in serch of Von.

This was my shape on first going out.

Sept 26th Layed by to day waiting for Whiteing who has not come up, his waggon and men are still with us — got an old long, gaunt, hipshot, sprained ankle bay mare from Sterns, She might, could, would or should have been a good animal one but her better days were past, and I knew as soon as I saw her that she would be, totally unfit for the long dry and tedious trip we were bent on. and more particularly for hunting &c, except to poke along very slowly which any one knows is tiresome to the rider. She was the only animal I could get however, and I consoled my self by taking the best I could get. went down the creek & killed some quails. and doves the only game I saw — one of the boys killed a hare We will soon be in a game country now however — and then —

Sept. 27th. Fixed up an old saddle tree, this morning Saddled my old mare 'Fashion' as I shall call her and we left old Sterns, and started for the Chow-chilla. Whiteing came up before we reached the chowchilla, bringing us the latest news from San Francisco, and some instructions from

my gun a few times before I could find out where it was, but at last I got an answer and a signal light upon one of the hills and carried the welcome news. we hitched up the mules and drove to the creek having made 24 miles to day — we found here the road that leds to Tular pass from the four creeks — we had to dig for water before we obtained it — I saw a great number of Tarantulas to day, and some of their singular nests or homes, it is very ingenious construction built of mud, and lined with a substance like the common spider web — and as smooth as satin or velvet. but the singularity is the door of his home which opens and shuts on a hinge, and when closed is not only water tight but air tight.

> *It is very ingenious construction built of mud and lined with a substance like the common spider web—and as smooth as satin or velvet, but the singularity is the door of his home which opens and shuts on a hinge, and when closed is not only water tight but air tight.*

"*OREORTYX PICTA*, MOUNTAIN QUAIL,"
ANDREW JACKSON GRAYSON, WATERCOLORS
OF BIRDS OF THE PACIFIC SLOPE.

trip, he and his old mare "Fashion" often took side trips in search of water, revelatory times for him to observe the dry land and its denizens. The grandiose title Grayson assigned to his tattered journal—"A Little Journal of Incidents whilst on a surveying party with 'Von Schmidt,' Deputy Surveyor under Col. Pack Hays in the fall of 1853, on the Tulare Plains"— suggests that he may have intended to rewrite it someday. He must have expected his family at least to read his accounts, as he bids them goodnight at the end of his entry for September 18.

Heinrich Biedermann

MARCH 22–MARCH 26, 1855

Heinrich Biedermann left his wife and children in Winterthur, Switzerland, in the 1850s and lived the life of a reasonably successful businessman in San Francisco and Oakland. In addition to his diary, the small collection of his papers in the library contains a purchase agreement for the "Sierra Nevada" mine, news clippings from the German-language *California Demokrat*, some correspondence, and an illustrated Chinatown food wrapper. ❖ He writes in Sütterlin, a handwritten form of German Blackletter, and masks some script in a seemingly indecipherable code, possibly shorthand. The entries, though prosaic, portray the frenetic workday of an intrepid young entrepreneur taking advantage of business opportunities wherever they may appear. He records that Thursday the 22nd of March was clear and cold. He was visited by his friend Sturzennegger, who wanted to build an orphanage but had recently lost his shirt. Müller arrived after 2 p.m. and confided that he would like to open a brewery but worried that his poor health would prevent it. In the evening Biedermann picked up Kellersberger's wife and child. On page 37 Biedermann lays out a business plan for purchasing a ship, hiring a captain and crew, hauling freight for a round trip of ten months, and then selling the ship at a profit. He remarks that a few carpenters bought an old ship for eight hundred dollars to fix up down at the wharf and sell in two months' time for three thousand.

" A few years ago Sturzennegger could have had $200.00 to build an orphanage in Watzenhausen, but he wanted more. Now he doesn't have anything. "

36. 1855. März.

J. Kellersberger, Surveyor
Broad Way, Oakland. 4½ Uhr

Maru von H. Müller.

22. Donnerstag. +10° Nsch.

[handwritten diary text, German Kurrentschrift, largely illegible]

1855. März.

B. Bischofberger
Adr. A. C. Rudig, Schwz. Consul
Valparaiso (Chili).

[handwritten text and accounts, German Kurrentschrift, largely illegible]

Stephen Wing

NOVEMBER 10, 1858

Mandalas and exquisite lettering decorate the cheerful entries of Stephen Wing's four California journals. Wing writes out his name in ornamented script in different inks many times, often filling a page with repetitions and variations on the theme and always, in the beginning, including the name of his hometown, South Yarmouth, Massachusetts. The word "Sunday" is also an opportunity for him to detour from the routine, lending it his full calligraphic repertoire, and he usually treats the day as special as his script. There isn't evidence in the text that suggests that Wing used mandalas as psychoanalyst C. J. Jung did in his own journals, as meditative cosmic diagrams, "cryptograms on the state of my self," but Wing labored over them, treasured them, and made them beautiful. ❧ Wing later prepared a series of lectures on his experiences in the West, derived no doubt from portions of his diaries. Would-be diarists may believe their lives lack events or scenes worthy of being recorded or sketched, but it is frequently in the description of small pleasures found in one's immediate surroundings, and in observances of the common and mundane, that a jewel-like existence is discovered.

> *Partner and I paid our store bill of provisions this day amt. $69.25 + Beef Bill = $75.00. My private bill at Wood's amounted to $28.50 which I paid also—money goes out full as fast as it comes in I find to my cost! Bought a claim this evening of Tweedy for $15.00. It is on Shingle Creek nearly opposite our cabin.*

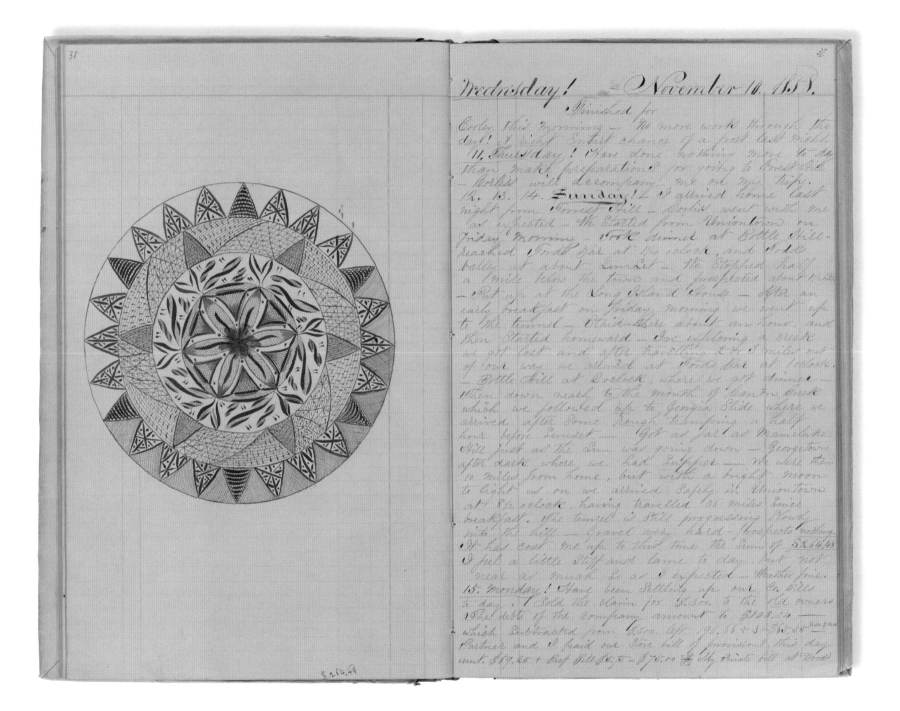

$264.48

Wednesday! — November 10. 1858.

Finished for
Cooley this morning — No more work through the
day! At night Smart chance of a frost last night.
11. Thursday! I have done nothing more to day
than make preparations for going to Forest Hill
— Corliss will accompany me on my trip.
12. 13. 14. Sunday! I arrived home last
night from Forrest Hill — Corliss went with me
as expected — We started from Uniontown on
Friday morning — took dinner at Bottle Hill —
reached Todds Bar at 1½ oclock, and Todds
valley at about Sunset — We stopped half
a mile below the town and prospected about 1½ hr
— Put up at the Long Island House — After an
early breakfast on Friday morning we went up
to the tunnel — Staid there about one hour, and
then started homeward — In exploring a creek
we got lost and after travelling 2 or 3 miles out
of our way we arrived at Todds Bar at 11 oclock.
— Bottle Hill at 2 oclock, where we got dinner —
then down nearly to the mouth of Canon Creek
which we followed up to Georgia Slide where we
arrived after some rough tramping a half
hour before Sunset — Got as far as Mameluke
Hill just as the Sun was going down — Georgetown
after dark where we had Supper — We were then
10 miles from home, but with a bright moon
to light us on we arrived safely in Uniontown
at 8½ oclock, having travelled 36 miles since
breakfast. the tunnel is still progressing slowly
into the hill — Gravel very hard — prospects nothing.
It has cost me up to this time the Sum of $264.48
I feel a little stiff and lame to day, but not
near as much So as I expected — Weather fine.
15. Monday! Have been settling up our Co. bills
to day. I Sold the claim for $.50. to the old owners
The debts of the company amount to $103.34 —
which Subtracted from $200. left $96.66 ÷ 3 = $36.55 —
Partner and I paid our Store bill & provisions this day
amt. $69.25 + Beef Bill $5.75 = $75.00 & My private bill at Todds

William Henry Brewer

FEBRUARY 19, 1861

William Brewer grew up on a New York farm, fascinated by plants, weather, and geology. He earned a degree in agricultural chemistry from Yale in 1852 and began teaching so that he could be free to travel in the summertime. When he was thirty-two and reeling from the death of his wife and infant son, he was recruited by newly appointed State Geologist Josiah Whitney for the fledgling California Geological Survey, which was to be an independent nonpolitical assessment of the region's natural resources. Brewer was Whitney's first appointment and proved an invaluable one, being "of the strongest fiber, of unflagging energy, the soundest judgment, the utmost tact, of unequivocal honesty, with a genial quality, and a keen and careful observer able to recognize the relative significance of things." A practical man, he was able to provide good-humored leadership in the field, fix a broken wagon wheel, repair a barometer, and round up mules gone astray. In the midst of prodigious activity, an endemic dearth of shelter, supplies, and food ("flour all gone, jerked beef ditto, onions ditto, potatoes ditto—long ago—have forgotten how some of them looked"),

" Went E. of camp about 2 miles, then struck north of camp over the hills—sandstone everywhere, in places traversed by thin veins of limestone, finely banded, but often crystalline. "

1862

Field Diary

and

Memoranda

Brewer

back in the hills, but were
seen rising above the front
tiers of hills. In the stream
found several sulphur springs,
some quite strong, and tasting
as if a considerable of
alkaline sulphurets were
held in solution. All the
water found along the base
of these hills is reported
bad, and is scarce. The soil
is cracking and baking in
the Sun. Rode back outside
of some of the foothills, and
inside of others.

After dinner examined
the sandstone outcropping to
the east of Camp. Some
characteristics were noticed
above. One large dome shaped
mass rising from near the base
of the hills, its sides worn into
castellate form. Many huge boulders

have rolled from it, one sketched
above was 40 or more ft high, and 152 in
circumference, another one measured
was 137 in circumference and at least
35 high. The weathering of this stone
into fantastic or grotesque forms
was shown in a rock of which the
following is an attempted sketch.

a large mass is priseo or two
slender legs leaning against a third

WILLIAM H. BREWER, SAN FRANCISCO, 1861,
BANCROFT PORTRAIT COLLECTION.

and in all kinds of inhospitable weather, he found time to keep several distinct sets of notebooks and diaries, to prepare detailed scientific reports, and to write the entertaining and comprehensive letters that he sent to his brother Edgar. Extrapolations and elaborations on his diaries, the letters created a composite journal of his four years on the survey. These were prepared for publication as *Up and Down California, 1860–1864* by Francis Farquhar in 1930. ❧ Brewer recorded in his notebooks everything he saw, with minute punctiliousness and an indefatigable curiosity. He even tasted the water to decipher its mineral content. When the workday was done, he would frequently climb the hill again, alone, just to watch the sunset or because the ceanothus was particularly lovely that evening. He appreciated a well-shaped oak, gifts of fruit from farms they traversed, and an especially comfortable campsite. Though his pages are written in light pencil and difficult to read, they are invaluable for the information they carry: weather statistics; estimates of distances, with measurements; notes on land formations, botany, and fossils; sketches; maps; and laments on the tribulations of farmers. ❧ In the one hundred and fifty years since Brewer wrote the pages pictured here during the field party's foray into the Santa Susana Mountains north of Los Angeles, changes may seem to have obliterated all traces of the land he saw, but behind the fences and up the canyons, Brewer's vivid descriptions may aid in identifying the party's trail. ❧ The well-thumbed diary pages are often stained and imprinted by plants once inserted, and pages for later dates in 1861 are illustrated further with drawings of a house, a wagon, and horses, all done by a childish hand—diary illustrations supplied by a successive generation.

MEMBERS OF THE CALIFORNIA GEOLOGICAL SURVEY ON MOUNT DIABLO, 1862, BANCROFT PORTRAIT COLLECTION.

Joseph LeConte

FEBRUARY 19, 1865

At the outbreak of the Civil War, Joseph LeConte was professor of chemistry and geology at South Carolina College at Columbia. He and his brother John continued to teach until their students had all been conscripted into the Confederate army. Though they did not take up arms themselves, the LeConte brothers participated in the manufacture of medical supplies and gunpowder for the Confederacy in Columbia. When Sherman began his March to the Sea, LeConte was desperate to reach Liberty County, Georgia; his fourteen-year-old daughter, Sallie, was staying there with his sister on the family farm, which lay directly in the swath that the Union army was cutting to Savannah. He embarked on a clandestine rescue mission behind enemy lines, traveling by Confederate supply train, wagon, and on foot. Carrying no weapon or dispatch, he would nevertheless have been a prize captive of the Yankees because of his chemical contributions to the war effort. Hiding in forest and swamp, crossing winter rain-fed rivers where the bridges had been blown up, or anxiously waiting until the road was again free of Union soldiers, LeConte wrote in his journal day by day. Though his escapes were hair-raising, frequent, and narrow enough to astonish, LeConte's illustrations, drawn by the fugitive as he lay concealed, are humorous and witty, belying the constant danger, cold, hunger, despair, doubt in the Confederacy, and enforced inactivity that are expressed in his words. Finally he succeeded in reaching Sallie and his sister and took them out on an old horse and a broken wagon in the midst of fifteen hundred marauding Yankees. One early morning before the Union soldiers had arisen, LeConte remarked

JOSEPH LECONTE, 1878,
BANCROFT PORTRAIT COLLECTION.

103

had known there were any Yankees in the house at that time. I learned afterwards from Sandy that these horsemen came to our camp looking for us that same night about 12 O.C. which was soon after they left us.

I listened to their retreating foot steps untill they became faint, then rose — drew a long breath & went to see how Capt Green fared. "Can that small dark gray bundle be Capt Green?!" Or is it a good sized toad? If it is the Capt, then what has become of his long limbs?" I poked him with a stick. "Capt! is this you?" The gray bundle slowly stirred — lifted itself up and expanded itself to the altitude of 6 good english feet. My stick was a magic wand — It was more — it was the spear of Ithuriel. It had suddenly transformed that small shape= less bundle into Capt Green in his true lineaments and his majestic proportions — A little shaky about the knees, a little tremulous in voice, but otherwise quite natural — We — listened intensely for a little while — The trampling grew faint= er & fainter & ceased. "Dr, is not that talking I hear in the road a little ahead of us?" I listened and thought I could hear it too. "Had we not better leave the road & strike into the field?" "Agreed" — We struck into the field in a direction at right angles to the road untill we had gone about 200 yds and were entirely concealed by the darkness. — then down to the river — then by the river margin untill we came near

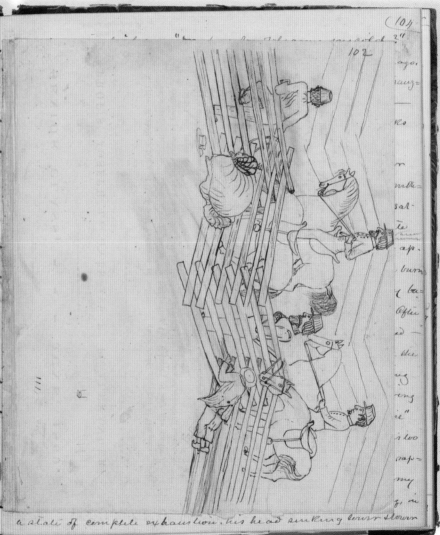

a state of complete exhaustion. His head sinking lower & lower

" I listened to their retreating footsteps until they became faint, then rose, drew a deep breath and went to see how Captain Green fared. "Can that small, dark grey bundle be Captain Green, or is it a gigantic toad? If it be indeed the Captain, what has become of his long legs?" **"**

with delight on the music of the whooping cranes and was glad that they had escaped the devastation. After two months, the family was reunited in Columbia, but five days later, as Sherman turned his attention to South Carolina, the brothers again left their families, this time on the university campus, trusting it would be safe from Yankee fire because of its status as a hospital, and fled to the surrounding countryside on orders from Richmond. Once again LeConte found himself hiding, this time in a dense quarter-acre of brambles and gallberry bushes, surrounded by Yankees intent on his capture. He managed to escape by the skin of his teeth again and again, more by luck than by skill. ❧ Living on the kindness of strangers and a peck of sweet potatoes roasted on a fence still smoldering from Yankee torches, LeConte writes and draws in his journal, pondering how one's senses are deceived in danger. Upon returning home again and discovering his house still standing and his family safe, he writes, "My life in the woods agreed with me astonishingly—I was never heartier in my life." ❧ After the war the LeConte brothers found every academic door closed against them because of their Confederate loyalty. But when word arrived of a new university on the Pacific Coast near San Francisco, they emigrated west. Joseph became professor of chemistry and geology, and his brother John professor of physics and astronomy at the new University of California. ❧ Historian Susanna Bryant Dakin wrote that "the LeConte Family was small in stature but lionhearted, one and all." In the entry pictured here, LeConte and his compatriot Capt. Green have just narrowly escaped detection by Union soldiers by hiding in the angles of a rail fence. Green is the gray "toad" on the left, wrapped in an old blanket.

Robert Nicholson Tate

FEBRUARY 25, 1873

Robert Tate's large ledger-book diary was written when he was older and
taking life slowly enough to notice the flowers in season and the social
events in the small Mississippi River town of Rock Island, Illinois, where he
farmed and grew grapes for his small winery. He had come to the United
States from England at the age of twenty-six and worked in partnership
with fellow blacksmith John Deere to build a plow factory in his earlier
years. He begins this diary by remarking with wonder that he is now the
age his father was when he died—sixty-seven. In this wonderful portrait of
a life well lived, Tate faithfully records each day's temperature and weather,
notes which flowers are in bloom—"trumpet flowers are flourishing
today"—and lovingly describes the business of running a home and farm.
He tells of making wild mushroom catsup, gathering honey, gooseberries,
and quinces—"pity poor Moses' boy who thought them pears!" He forgives
loans, scrapes off kitchen wallpaper, cleans the cistern, lays in cords of wood,
notices shooting stars, and takes home curious insects to study under the
microscope. Duly noted are the tasks of training grapevines to trellises and
measuring the sugar content of the grapes. He keeps a pet flying squirrel
and exults in the first strawberry blossom and a day of good sleighing
snow. This small-town Renaissance man reports on the circuses, fairs, and
Mississippi River boat races that come to town, and he reads Shakespeare
and paints during the quiet days of winter. His journal also lists his

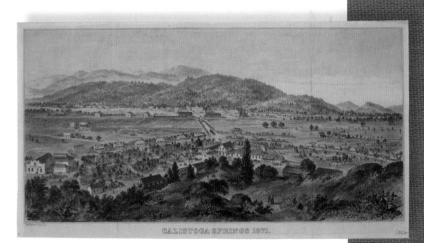

"Calistoga Springs," Britton and Rey, 1871, Honeyman
collection of early Californian and Western
American pictorial material.

Feby 25"

Remarks For 1873.

There is a fountain in the center of the plaza — but to all appearance it was not fountain much lately a repository for the dead having 6 cells about 30 square. The whole Structure is about 12 feet square one inscription was Maria Jesus Lergo De Williams Born June 21" 1820. Died June 28" 1842 in one of such a place in which there had been interred the body of a child about 10 year old & as part of the Masonry had fallen out exposing the end of the coffin I look in the the coffin lid was removed & the lining torn to shreds by a piece of ground Squareel infest every place I have seen on the Pacific for 600 miles they were not in the graveyards last that I know of, but here they are a pest i—e if people thought so But that's a question all over the country & people eat these pests they don't leave a bone of all & every buried person if a wood coffin encloses the body they have no difficulty at all they can go right into it the very day they are interred & these pests are in every field garden & lot used in fact they are a pest they are active & destructive Ermin—

This is another on same plan with on large opening — a popular tree either intentionally or otherwise kept in front of the opening in which they had long before put the coffin as the tree completely blenk't up at this time no inscription that I could discover & only intended for one coffin there were a great many such of various sizes & patterns some of them split from top to bottom the grave yard contained from 15 to 20 acres & was pickeled & whitewash — after passing this cemetry, a huge water wheel loom up in the distance b as the view is not obstructed for 50 or 60 miles away this Structure with its numerous ribs radiating from center to circumference appeared very distinctly I soon was on the platform beneath this huge city appendage for at one time it must have supplied them with water in this wheel there are 32 buckets each about 26 feet from the center each bucket is loaded with 100 each holding about 12½ gallons of water measuring 3476 square inches there is invariably every bucket invisit from square barrels .... So that when the bucket is full the are empty

1873 Remarks For 1873.

Feby 25" This mill is about 1½ miles from Pico House

This Mill is about 1½ miles from the Pico Building. Between which there a several Brick yard & they make as good Brick as ever I saw the Clay is excelent There is an Enclosure in which the French Council installs himself it is allso an hospital & Retreat for French invalids the of Loss Angeles 160 feet in this garden contains fine Specimens of young oranges & Lemons here I saw the best bearing young orchard I have seen yet the Limons are large & rather clumsey looking fruit. Continued from page 83½ my remarks don't afraid me much of any logs from this untill we get to point concep on which there is a light house after rounding this headland we took we took a straight shoot for Santa Barbra, there are three large Islands in the bay about 25 miles from the coast consequently this passage — between the island & the main land is called Santa Barbra Channel, we touched at Santa Barbra & afterwards rounding the headland point Conception) we had little to do with the Shore we noticed quite a distinct difference in the water from light blue to yellow about noon on Wednesday about half way we rounded a point of land. The current setting strong from the north swept in & out of this Bay this point is the first headland after we pass point Conception northwards the mate says we are to be at Sanfrancisco at ½ after 3 p m present present time ½ after 10 a m we have seen no fish No Seal No Sea weed we are now passing point An Neza Steaming away — passed this rocky point at ½ after 2 p m thurs Feby 27" we are wending our way into port very quiet

Sanfrancisco on entering the port

Goat Island

a view from there seaward on entering into the city

Sanfrancisco on entering the port

expenses, sometimes substantial, as when there was a fire in the glassworks upon which he depended for his wine bottles or when he sent a large donation to the sheriff to aid victims of the Great Chicago Fire in 1871. He is mildly surprised when the beer he laid in on April 23 is gone already by May 6, and thinks that Charley Dixon sold his good name to the highest bidder when he ran off with a wealthy widow. ❧ In July 1873, with his wife, Margaret, and youngest daughter, Emma, Tate boarded a train on the Rock Island Line for the five-day journey to California to visit his grown children, Anna in Calistoga and William in Santa Rosa, both struggling to make a living by farming and to raise children past infancy. When Emma chose to remain in California to teach school, her parents decided to stay as well and briefly considered purchasing an orange orchard. Tate helped his children on their farms, picking fruit and gathering wool. In his diary he comments on grapevines and winemaking in California and worries when the expanding towns replace vineyards and farms. In July of 1873 he and Margaret traveled to Los Angeles to visit Emma in her new job, staying downtown near the Pico House. He writes of the locals, "Their horses are homely, and they seem to be very partial to pigeons." On the pages reproduced here, he describes his impressions of the Plaza in Los Angeles. Later he had a studio on Post Street in San Francisco and made a modest name for himself as a painter of portraits and Napa Valley landscapes. Other Tate diaries are in the John Deere and University of Illinois archives.

> "As part of the masonry had fallen out exposing the end of the coffin, I look[ed] in. The coffin lid was removed and the lining torn to shreds by a species of ground squirrel that infest every place I have seen on the Pacific for 600 miles. They were not in the graveyards last that I know of, but here they are a pest."

Caroline Eaton LeConte

JULY 3, 1878

"Professor Joe" LeConte spent a long summer's month in 1878 camping in Yosemite Valley and the Calaveras Grove of giant sequoias, accompanied by his wife, Bessie, fourteen-year-old daughter, Caroline ("Carrie"), and nine-year-old son, Little Joe. Also along were Carrie's best friend, Nona Dibble, Joseph's dandyish friend Lieutenant Greenough, "mild-eyed, melancholy, rice-eating" Lee the cantankerous cook, and the dashing but dense, egg-loving student Charlie Butters to drive the green and red painted wagon—a large congenial party of eight. Precocious Carrie filled two volumes with her descriptions of the people they met, their hilarious conversations, and the escapades they had. In these "Adventures of N & C," she pens picturesque portraits of each of the members of their group, including the eccentric horses: Royal Arches, named for his "gaunt backbone like the highest ridge of the Sierras"; the voracious Longitude, with "an enormously long body like a stuffed lobster"; pampered, preening Dick; and the white beast ridden by Professor Joe, the pesky Geological Mule who never lost a trail. "Mr. Butters gives his whip a flourish, and the horses start off with a merry jingle and 'tinpanabulations' from a couple of tin cans and a dangling coffee-pot accompanied by the agreeable thump-thump and rattle of the tent poles." Nona and Carrie spend their days bathing in the frigid waters of their Azalea Pool on the Merced River, planning excursions, "discovering" new landmarks, visiting the waterfalls, and poking fun at "the hotel people" who disdain the unkempt campers. They get up before dawn to hike to Mirror Lake to see the reflections before the wind rises to ruffle the surface, read George Eliot in the canvas tent, and eagerly anticipate the

CAROLINE EATON LeCONTE, 1883,
BANCROFT PORTRAIT COLLECTION.

1. The "Tony" ministers
3. That meek looking youth yclept "Jack." 2. Artist.
4. Stout Lady. 5. An old lady who was riding in "Bloomer" costume (This is a fact)
6. A sweet young thing.

needles. "Poor things!" I said, "they don't have any nice times at all; they don't ever climb after Tent Rocks and slide down boulders, they don't scramble up near the falls, they don't bathe in the Merced river, they don't ride on little white mules, they don't have camp fires! I wonder if the "poor hotel people" didn't pity us too? Here is a picture I drew of a party of hotel people admiring Bridal Veil Fall in the distance and by the help of opera-glasses and guide books: in the rear, the head of the

> "Come now," said Mr. Butters with beaming eyes, ladling out the milk as fast as he could, "don't let's let all this fine milk go to waste." "Don't be afraid," returned the Lieutenant with a sort of choking gurgle in his throat, "it'll all go to waist anyhow."

evening campfires. Carrie's journal was lost from out of the wagon several times during the trip, inspiring Mr. Butters to exasperatedly call it "that old abominably interminable note-book," but with great relief someone always found it in the end. Carrie's niece later remembered her aunt as "a wonderful storyteller," and artist and family friend William Keith regarded her as a gifted writer with "more soul than body."

Samuel Clemens (Mark Twain)

JANUARY 4, 1879

When he was nineteen, Samuel Clemens first began carrying a notebook with him, entering "French lessons, phrenological information, miscellaneous observations, and reminders about errands to be performed." The notebooks he would keep throughout his life followed this same random form. He used them to record ideas and notes when he was a newspaper correspondent and later as fodder and inspiration for his longer literary works, many of which were travel books. "It is a troublesome thing for a lazy man to take notes, and so I used to try in my young days to pack my impressions in my head. But that can't be done satisfactorily, and so I went from that to another stage—that of making notes in a note-book. But I jotted them down in so skeleton a form that they did not bring back to me what it was I wanted them to furnish. Having discovered that defect, I have mended my ways a good deal in this respect, but still my notes are inadequate. However, there may be some advantage to the reader in this, since in the absence of notes imagination has often to supply the place of facts." ❧ In Clemens's seventeenth journal, he is traveling through Germany, Switzerland, Italy, France, Belgium, Holland, and England in 1878, with the rather unhappy intention of writing "the troublesome book," *A Tramp Abroad*, but not enjoying it much. He characterizes the book as written "by one loafer for a brother loafer to read," but he also avows that "I *hate* to travel, & I *hate* hotels, & I *hate* the opera, & I *hate* the Old Masters." If, as Ralph Ellison wrote of Mark Twain, "He made it possible for many of us to find our own voices," then Twain's journals may be read as singing lessons.

> " *Miss Benfey said: "Very great singer,— one of our greatest—but hasn't any voice these last 10 yrs—but he must sing once a year to keep his pension."* "

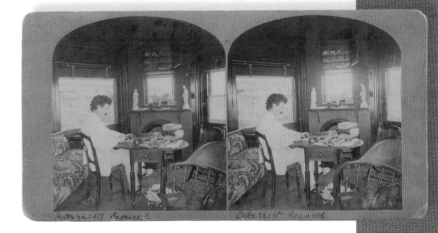

SAMUEL L. CLEMENS, QUARRY FARM STUDIO, 1874, MARK TWAIN PAPERS AND PROJECT.

Throw in some oil
(Pennsylvania coal oil)

Say, I made a little
sketch, &c.

Washington + my Delaware

Colosseum

Parthenon

Heidelberg Castle.
Grand Canal, Venice
San Marco & Square

St Marks

LION of St. MARK.

Miss Benfey, said:
Niemann is our best
singer but he has no
voice — ie is a splendid
actor & once had a noble
voice. (Trouble with all of 'em
here

"Very great singer,
— one of our greatest, —
but hasn't any voice
these last 10 yrs — but
he must sing once a
year to keep his pension"
"He not sing, he cry"

John Muir

MID-JULY, 1879

"I went to see glaciers, etc.," writes John Muir in 1879 while on the first of his seven trips to Alaska, but his diary tells of much more than ice flows. A diarist for forty-four years, Muir first wrote and drew pictures in a journal in 1867 as he tramped through the American South, including a self-portrait while camped among the graves in the Buenaventura Cemetery in Savannah. A young man off to see the world, he wrote on the flyleaf his name and address, "John Muir, Earth-Planet, Universe." He generally used a dull pencil to write in his ever-present notebooks and often did not date his entries. He believed that he wrote more freely in his journals than when he was writing down his thoughts—"dead bone-heaps"—for publication, but felt that putting more of himself into the writing would "spoil their symmetry with mere trials and adventures." ❖ Muir's first trip to Alaska began on July 10, 1879, on the mail steamer *California* and was intended to be a month in duration, to solve the unanswered questions related to his theory of glaciation in the Sierra Nevada. But taking numerous side trips, entranced with the Alaskan summer days and the "small bare rocks like black dots, mere specks, punctuating the end of a grand, eloquent, on-swelling sentence of islands tree-laden; all reflected in mirror-blue water, forms and meaning doubled," he repeatedly missed ships headed south and didn't reach home for another six months. ❖ Muir's writing is a jeweled chain of word pictures—"a tepid, drizzling, leaf-making day"—with scarcely a need for illustration, but he graces nearly every page with drawings that evoke the "finest and freshest landscape poetry on the face of the globe." Already he sees that Alaska is in danger from exploitation. "The difficulty in the way of those who regard every uneaten and unsold

"Our whistle-screams and cannon-shot awakened the boggy village, and down came a score or two of Indians and a half-dozen whites to the end of the wharf ere we were alongside. The Captain assured us we should find it a miserable place built in a swamp, no good thing about it or in it; only looked well to him over the stern of his ship when leaving it."

64

I had ere this sought for work in all
the mills. & thought of setting out for the fields
to pick cotton, or steal corn.

On the sixth day I bade a last
farewell to Bonaventure & to all its
glories, held a jubilee of bread
& took passage in the steamer Sylvan
Shore for Fernandina, & thus handsomely terminated my "marching
through Georgia." The agent
at last said, Yes, the money has
come but how am I
to know You

{ My Bonaventure home }

are John Muir, I said I know
nobody here to identify me, but
look at this letter telling how
much is sent by whom &
to whom he said Yes that

goldenrods & dwarf palmettos. Florida.   77

is good as far as it goes but
how am I to know that
you have not stolen J. Muir's
letter. I said Well I suppose
from him to school
you know something of
botany. Now the letter says
that the writer wishes I
having a good
botanical time. & find my
new plants as
many of I could steal
a letter from
John Muir & I could
not steal his botany by Mr & —

{ Saw Palmetto, & wand Solidago etc
Southern Georgia & Florida-ab. }

This palmlet is very abundant in every
moderately dry & open place in Florida pre-
fering the "Pine barrens" sandy & shelly correly
places. The leaves are perfect fans in

Back of Sitka, looking E.

fish and every unsawn tree in the woods, and every dollar's worth of mineral in the mountains, as lost and worthless, is that all of these may yet be found in more accessible portions of our big country." "While we sail on and on through the infinite beauty enchanted, hard, money-gaining, material thoughts loosen and sink off and out of sight, and one is free from oneself and made captive to fresh wildness and beauty, obeying it as necessarily as unconscious sun-bathed plants." The key to such reveries of course is taking time, stopping to notice a lovely bog "covered with beautiful mosses and alpine flowers" yet dismissed by a fellow passenger as a miserable swamp, or to experience the aftermath of an avalanche—"zigzags of silvery cascades." Muir enriched the world when he took the time to sit "on the bulging mossy roots of an old hemlock…while daylight still lingered" to observe and record in his journals the sights, sounds, and living things of Alaska in 1879, from the massive peaks down to the small fly that he drew in the margin of one of the pages.

JOHN MUIR, BANCROFT PORTRAIT COLLECTION.

Joshua Elliott Clayton

AUGUST 1, 1879

A self-taught mining engineer who began working in the early 1840s, J. E. Clayton had accumulated nearly fifty years of practical experience by the time of his death. Though he was unschooled in the universities of his time, his expertise, analyses, innovation, and inventions were highly regarded throughout the country. An omnivorous reader and student of nature, he was content to take off on his own, needing no more than his hand hammer, magnifying glass, and a pile of shells and rocks to make him happy. Furious at the "sharpers and unprincipled men [who] for selfish and dishonest purposes" deluded miners "with plug hats and store clothes, without pick and shovel" to lose their shirts in the Gold Rush, Clayton steadfastly believed that there were "a few honorable men yet left in California" to work with him on a plan to develop technology so that an enduring industry could be built in the state, saving it "from the charge of humbuggery." ❖ Heavily illustrated with cross sections of earth, profiles of above-ground formations, water access, tunnel diagrams, and equipment, his journals contain notes for his testimony as an expert witness in mine-related litigation, ideas for journal articles, notes from his examinations of mines for potential buyers, and notes for the promotion of mineral properties, but also his impatience with the "greediness and stubbornness" of others in the field. Clayton insisted that he would deal only with reputable men—"I intend to see that my parties get *good* mines at *fair* prices"—which may be the reason that although he was widely respected and admired, he "made but a doubtful living" in the West. He died in a stagecoach accident near Helena, Montana, in 1889 when his driver began racing a second coach.

JOSHUA ELLIOTT CLAYTON, BANCROFT PORTRAIT COLLECTION.

Eureka Aug 1st 1879

Stella Mine - 200 × 800

Situated on west side of
New York canon and halfway
up E. face of N.Y. Hill

Shaft at N End 20 ft deep
on Pipe of ore 4 to 6 ft. Dia—
appears to be an irregular pipe
of good quartzey ore—

near S end an open
cut 30 ft long 10 ft deep
also a tunnel 75 ft
connected by a chute
about 80 tons of
quartz on dumps
and in Tunnel
all low grade, used
for flux at Rich
mond furnaces

a system of gash seams and ore
pipes in sandy limestone and
quartzose masses in same

Shaft at N End 20 ft deep on Pipe of ore 4 to 6 ft. Dia—appears to be an irregular pipe of good quartzey ore.

Amos Batchelder

MAY 4–MAY 9, 1886

A sparsely worded diary can well evoke a bountiful life. Dr. Amos Batchelder kept a diary of his overland journey to California in 1849 and a notebook of medical prescriptions, but it is the journal he kept in 1886 that is so revealing of the man and his times. There is biography between the lines and in the small drawings that adorn each entry. Written in his home in Pelham, New Hampshire, and begun on New Year's Day with a self-portrait, the diary portrays the solitary life of a rather lonely country doctor—"No patients came today"—who nevertheless delights in the birds and plants he sees every day. His wife has died, and his children have moved away. In his simple summations of each day, Dr. Batchelder shines a light on the Spartan, sensitive New England existence of an older adult. His daily drawings represent small pleasures and observances in his immediate surroundings and are reminiscent of Dan Price's words in *The Moonlight Chronicles*, "To draw everything is saying things no one can hear."

"Fine weather with signs of a storm. Charles and Warren Kent plowed N.E. quarter of upper field and got out manure. Gardening some carrots and beets sown. My brother William died this afternoon."

Ther. **TUES. MAY 4, 1886** Wea.

Warmer than yesterday.
Ground getting very dry.
John got manure on to
garden and plowed it.
Doing not much myself

Ther. **WEDNESDAY 5** Wea.

Warmer and somewhat
muggy. Thunder shower
here for the first time
this season. Onions and
parsnips sown to day.
Peas, Gladiolus Japan lilly.
Geraniums put in the ground

Ther. **THURSDAY 6** Wea.

Very fine day and warm.

Three ladies to see museum
Worked in carriage house

Ther. **FRI. MAY 7, 1886** Wea.

Fine weather with signs
of a storm.
Charles and Warren Kent
plowed N.E. quarter of
upper field and got out
manure. Gardening some
Carrots and beets sown
My Brother William died
this afternoon

Ther. **SATURDAY 8** Wea.

North east rain storm.
Rainy all day. Face of
nature much improved
by it. Worked in carriage
house

Ther. **SUNDAY 9** Wea.

Cool North west wind.
Still warm and pleasant
in the evening. with new
moon 6 days old.
Trees are blossoming. and
every thing looks fresh
and fine.

Mary Robertson Bradbury

SEPTEMBER 17, 1886

Many oceangoing diary entries tell of the agonies of seasickness, but few are as evocative of the condition as the drawing of "Mrs. W., as seen crossing the Channel." A recent graduate of the Art Students League in New York City, Mary Bradbury was twenty-one when she made the trans-Atlantic crossing in winter to continue her studies in Europe. She also made daily progress reports on a printed map, a "Passengers' Track Chart" provided by the Guion Line U.S. Mail Steamer Company that she carried inside the cover of her journal. It is apparent that she is experimenting, nurturing a habit of observation and expression. Assigning them nicknames such as Mr. Plum Pudding and Little Boss, she writes witty descriptions of her fellow travelers—

" At St. Augustine's Monastery, the verger gave us a bit of the tile forming mosaic in the old floor. He said, "I should not do it, you know," with a charming smile. "

"a laugh like a bottle of Vichy going off"—and also uses her diary as an autograph book, asking some she meets to write in it. She finds Paris "delicious! such sights, such shops such brilliancy, everybody happy, smiles and absinthe at every corner!" Thrilled by all she sees, she is disappointed that everyone she meets knows immediately that she is an American. Yet in Spain she and her friend Charles are taken for magicians and French spies because they are sketching *en plein air* and because Mary has a gold tooth, "el molar d'oro!" She is irritated by Charles's insatiable collecting of clocks and that he eats "all day till he grows as round as a partridge." At the end of the trip, delayed in dreary wintry London nearly a month, Bradbury spends her days sketching "till the hail and rain came down so hard that my subject was blotted from sight." ❖ Bradbury married architect John Galen Howard in New York in 1893, moved to California with him in 1902, and continued to paint in an Impressionist manner when she could find the time. ❖ Missing from the lower left corner of this page is the piece of the sheltering yew tree given to her by the verger of St. Martin's Church in Canterbury before she left England. Many of the diary pages bear imprints and shadows of the blossoms, sprigs, and tickets that were later removed.

you American ladies!" this is an example
of English high born manners, & of the
"blarney" of the lower classes -
We learn that our host & hostess were
formerly of the Duke of Beaufort's household. Our informant said "they have seen
✗ the best society."
At S. Augustine's Monastry, the verger
gave us a bit of the tile forming mosaic
in the old floor - he said "I should not do
it, you know," with a charming smile.
Asked for young Fothergill, & found him
as like his father - a charming fellow -
he showed us his rooms, an honor we
appreciated, & was very agreeable. I
caused the greatest excitement by standing
with my back against a house & sketching
in the street - such fun!

bit of yew tree - 600 yrs.
from S. Martin's
Canterbury.

Sep.17 - Crossing the Channel to Calais -
First intimation of French - perfectly
indistinguishable - hopeless -

Mrs. W. as seen crossing the Channel.
Paris - Hotel de Lamballe rue Richepanse
The ride through Brittany rather uninter-
esting - the country wears a dingy look -
very different from brilliant England -
crops, colours & peasants all sober &
subdued. peculiar trees, very picturesque - charming glimpses of walled
chateaux, white plaster & thatched roofs -
the most awfully uneven road I
ever travelled on - we went very fast
& shook up tremendously -

Joseph Nisbet LeConte

JULY 17 AND JULY 25, 1889

> *Little Jingle looked quite spry and plump after his long rest, and went about camp eating up all the paper and empty tin cans he could find. Finally he ate up my soap and oilcloth, so I tied him to a tree, where he consoled himself with a piece of tin foil.*

A third LeConte diarist was trailblazer and mapmaker Little Joe, son to Joseph and younger brother to Carrie. With his father and three fellow students, the "Jolly Jaunting Juniors," Little Joe set out July 1, 1889, on an ambitious, jubilant, six-week tour of Yosemite. Loading the reluctant horses in San Francisco onto a Stockton-bound steamer, the group then continued on a two-week trek southeast to Yosemite, stopping at farms along the way to stable the horses, to take relief in the shade from the 106 degree heat, to eat the gifts of eggs, figs, and milk, and sleep in the haylofts. When they at last reached Yosemite, the nineteen-year-olds were reckless with bravado, scampering up impossible slopes, skipping across slippery, rushing torrents, hurling boulders off precipices, yelling college songs from a speeding wagon, and wrestling in meadow grass, and they were scolded by Joseph for falling asleep on a narrow ledge thirty-seven hundred feet above the Yosemite Valley floor. They then headed east from the valley, cutting cross-country toward Tuolumne Meadows, from which they climbed to the summits of Mount Hoffman, Mount Dana, and Mount Lyell, all in just five days. Along the way they mocked the fool tourists, ate buckets of wild black raspberries, and snapped photos with an early Kodak camera. ❖ The following year, Little Joe kept a diary of another trip to the Sierra Nevada, this time in the company of three friends, a zither, a Kodak camera, barometric instruments, and three donkeys, Roxy, Jingle, and Jenny. The ensuing entries are as much about the adventures of the donkeys as they are

with him for he too is going, while
his "pardner" takes care of the mine. Tomorrow we will strike eastward. Everybody seems to be going in a bunch." As
Guy rode off we slowly returned to camp.
We four will have to fight it out alone
now. In the evening we set fire to a
dead oak, but the resulting bon-fire was
not a success. The old tree smouldered
all night, waking us every now and then
by the crash of a falling limb.

July 17

Got up early this morning
and packed up our things on the jacks
for leaving. Little Jingle looked quite spry
and plump after his long rest, and went
about camp eating up all the paper and
empty tin cans he could find. Finally he
ate up my soap and oilcloth, so I tied him
to a tree, where he consoled himself with
a piece of tin foil. Our packs are extremely
light, the 50 lb sack of flour bought from
Fox being the only heavy article. This is
a good thing as we will travel light

across the Kearsarge Pass." At 7 A.M. we
left our beautiful camp on the King's
River, and started up the well known
trail toward the mines." As I passed
the camp I looked about for the old
fellow to tell him good bye, but he was
not in. Soon a tremendous explosion that
sent the echoes flying down the cañon
told us that he was at work in his
mine blasting. Walked up the long trail
till near the junction of Bubbs Creek
and King's River. Here I discovered that
I had left the aneroid barometer behind.
It was a fine instrument worth $80. lent
me by a friend, so I gave my pack, the
camera, to the other boys and started
back in a hurry.

Sketch of the
Grand Cañon.
3 miles = about 2 inches.

128

1906/1

fore they came in. We had made the ascent
in 3 hours, they in 4. On the summit was
a large pile of rocks put up by some enter
prising climbers, and in the crevices were
innumerable tin cans filled with the names
of visitors. We looked through them all.
In one was a note left by the California
Geological Survey party who were the first
white men to set foot on the summit. Here
is a fac-simile of it, copied on the spot.

State Geological Survey

June 28th 1863—

J. D. Whitney

W. H. Brewer — Charles F. Hoffmann

ascended this mountain June 25th & again the
29th — We give the name of Mt DANA to it
in honor of J. D. Dana the most eminent Am
erican geologist. Approximate height 13,126 feet

Among others we found father's name. There was
a can reserved for University men, and in
this we "registered." Started down at 1:30. Went
striding down the loose rocks at a great rate

129

A stream of loose debris would start down
with us, and on this moving support we could
go 10 feet at a step. Oh but it was paralyzing
on shoes — to dig the heels into the sharp
slate. When I got to the saddle, all the leather
was torn off the back of my clod-hoppers, and
one sole was about to drop off. Palache and I
arrived in camp at 3 P.M.,
the others at 3:30. I
immediately set to work
to mend my shoes, which
I succeeded in doing
tolerably well. If they last
through the Lyell climb,
I'll be satisfied. Father
told us he had been
boiling a pot of beans
all day and they

Palache asleep on the summit of Dana

weren't done yet. — N.B. we were 10,100 feet above
the sea. We were in fine spirits that evening, not
in the least tired. In fact the climb was not
as hard as Mt Hoffmann. Built a tremendous
camp fire. The nights are very cold in this region,
and fires are necessary to sleep by. Today on
the summit of Dana our second roll of Kodak
film ran out, and we have no more. Too bad. Our

Time 3¾" wide

❝ Started down at 1:30. Went striding down the loose rocks at a great rate. A stream of loose debris would start down
with us, and on this moving support we could go 10 feet at a step. Oh, but it was paralyzing on shoes. ❞

about the antics and exploits of the four campers. This time, coaxing and beseeching the donkeys along, they went on foot east from Fresno to the Kings River, following it up over the foothills into the High Sierra. Fueling up on great quantities of pilot bread, "rib-sticker" flapjacks, gifts of mutton from shepherds, venison they shot, raspberries, and enormous quantities of trout, they made breathtakingly vertical ascents, killed seventeen rattlesnakes, and soothed their ailments with Jamaica ginger and whiskey. Little Joe went off on side trips to measure cliff heights, in his nascent efforts to map this wildest region. They were thrilled to find at one point that they were following in the footsteps of the California Geological Survey team. Inexhaustible, they hiked twenty-two miles in one day with a vertical ascent of five thousand feet, and on another, plunged down the Eastern Sierra to the Owens Valley, nine thousand feet in nine miles, only to climb west again up the Kern River Canyon to the summit of Mount Whitney. After descending again to the Owens Valley flatlands, the group turned around and crossed Mono Pass and circled Yosemite Valley via Glacier Point and Hetch Hetchy before reaching home nine weeks and seven hundred miles later. At the end of the tramp, Little Joe's shoes had no heels and little sole, and his clothes were "in the last stages of dilapidation." The men gave Roxy, Jingle, and Jenny to farms they passed on the route home, the little donkeys completely worn out with the trek. Little Joe later taught mechanical and hydraulic engineering, followed John Muir to become the second president of the Sierra Club in 1915, and continued to map the Sierra Nevada.

JOSEPH NISBET LECONTE, "PACKING UP AT HARDIN'S, 1893," BANCROFT PORTRAIT COLLECTION.

Mae Somers Peterson

MAY 21–MAY 23, 1891

"I came up from lunch today. Fannie was holding him in her arms—when he saw me he threw his arms up, gave a little spring, and made a little glad noise as though he were overjoyed to see me."

Every page of a baby book or memory book is filled with wonder and amazement as each new developmental milestone is reached, each new tooth is spotted, and each wobbly adventurous step is taken. Each memory-book child is the sharp focus of a devoted parent, and is usually the firstborn. Each of them is astonishingly talented and exceptionally good—exactly as it should be. The diaries become treasured mementos of days soon forgotten in the blur and hustle of growing up. Baby F. Somers Peterson was named three months after his birth in 1891 after his father, Ferdinand, but was called Somers because "we do not want Old Ferd and Young Ferd." In the diary, however, he is simply called Baby. The scion of an alliance of venerable and socially prominent San Francisco families, Baby was dressed in white fur-collared silk and white kid moccasins, and he learned to speak French from Pauline, his French nurse, but he began to crawl backwards and amused himself for hours with a simple rattle just like any little one. His mother, Mae, made short and infrequent entries in Baby's book but when his little sister, Kate (Peterson Mailliard), was born in 1892, the entries ceased altogether. In fact, they ceased mid-word and mid-sentence: "Took the two children to spen…" So many occupations are begun with best intentions, but forgotten within three days—diets and diaries foremost among them. Mae Peterson wrote well past that third-day hurdle.

Hair cut off.
May 21st 91

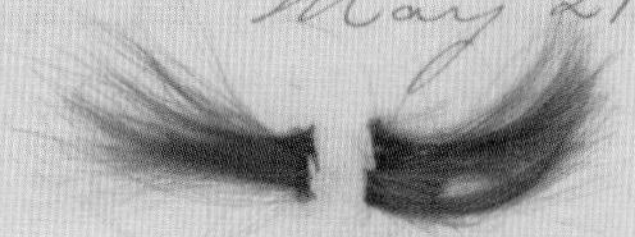

His first Hair

May 22nd

We came over to
Berkeley this afternoon to
spend a week.   When
we arrived here Mama
took the boy and began to
talk to him and he
laughed out loud for the
first time. He laughed
and laughed.

May 23rd

We took the eight thirty
train for S.F. — the 9.30
for Fairfax. had lunch
at Mrs. Roys. The baby was
exceptionally good all day.

Julia Mann Barr

SEPTEMBER 26–SEPTEMBER 30, 1902

Doris Barr was born in 1901 to adoring parents. Her mother, Julia, had been a teacher but left her job when she married her school superintendent. Doris recalled later in her life that Julia "was really only interested in her home and family," and that she had been "a shy, sensitive person, deaf since her early thirties." Doris thought that these qualities had much to do with her being a homebody and a devoted parent. Julia began the "life books" when Doris was born, and the tradition continued until 1935, filling nineteen volumes. Around volume four, Doris took over, supplementing her entries with photographs, clippings, and memorabilia. When she was eleven, her father became the Director of Congresses at the Panama-Pacific International Exposition, and the family lived within the grounds of the fair. "I wandered at will with my notebook describing all the exhibits." When she was hungry, she would buy a Scotch scone dripping with strawberry jam for a nickel and help herself to free samples of olives. It was there too that she fell in love for the first time, with the elevator boy of the Inside Inn. The diaries follow Doris to new abodes, on family vacations, through school, and into her professions as a soprano and importer of Italian art objects. When Doris and her husband, Dan Stanislawski, had children of their own, Julia once again began "life books," this time for her two grandchildren, Anna and Michael, and these make the final two volumes of the set.

JULIA MANN BARR, PHOTOGRAPHS FROM DORIS BARR STANISLAWSKI'S LIFE BOOKS.

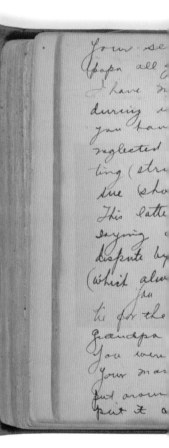

building continues. Now it is papa-all-dawn
stead of simply "aw-dawn."

you using so many new words
...k. This list also includes some which
... using for a month but which I have
... : hair - fire - chick - n - swee sweet, —
... pē (Bo Beef) - tock n (stocking) bā (back)
... (write) - pē-pē (pencil) — tow (cow) hā (horse)
... your papa insisted you were not
... argued that you were. You settled the
... hā and then giving the clucking sound
... horse with your immediately after.
... door very plainly, also tie. You used
... time this morning. We went down to
... to breakfast because papa was in it.
... in that old fashioned high chair which
... when she was a baby and a cloth
... with tied to tie you in. As aunt Hattie
... you, you surprised us by saying tie.

seems sweeter than the last.

...re pictures which
Webster of Oakland took of
you arrived today. We are
more than pleased with them.
Those fine quaint little
figures we think are just
as sweet
as they
can possi-
bly be.
Some
look at
them each
picture

September 30, 1902
A year and a half old today
your mama asked you this
afternoon if you wanted a ride on the street car.
You were very happy then and kept saying
"tee tar" all the while I was putting on your
white dress and your white shoes and stockings.

“Your mama asked you this afternoon if you wanted a ride on the street car. You were very happy then and kept
saying "tee tar" all the while I was putting on your white dress and your white shoes and stockings.”

Jessie Colmer

APRIL 9, 1908

The chapters comprising Jessie Colmer's diary of her round-the-world trip were gathered and bound into a volume for her by her brother, "with much love," a year after her return. With the help of Thomas Cook travel agents, Colmer set out from Bournemouth, England, on the complicated thirteen-month ship-to-ship chain of connections that would take her to France, Spain, Barbados, Trinidad (where she visited relatives), Panama, Mexico, San Francisco (shortly after the 1906 earthquake and fire), Hawai'i, Japan, China, Australia, Sri Lanka, the Suez Canal, Gibraltar, and home to England. She sent the installments from the various ports where she disembarked, avowing that her efforts at writing were poor, and that she had no clever or witty things to say. Dismissing the social events and card games that happened down below, she preferred to be on deck whenever possible, wrapped

> " *Then there is a priest of very comely proportions, whose sole occupation is eating and sprawling in a hammock chair with his treble chin resting on his cushioned breast and his eyes closed in blissful meditation.* "

in fur coat and rug, with her "hot jar" and sealskin jacket. "I like my chair put to the *lowest* notch—that's all!" Occasionally she would succumb to a companionable tea or game of chess with her fellow passengers, but most days and some nights would find her topside, swaddled and busy with her watercolors, her diary, and her watching of "the sapphire sea." Much delayed by quarantines for yellow fever and plague, she was an intrepid tourist who managed to make the most of her connections and sought out places to stay on land with no advance reservations. Colmer found fault with some of the food at sea—"The butter is not nice!"—but was in awe of the courteous staff of the San Francisco post office. She considered the foliage of Hawai'i in better condition than that of Trinidad. She didn't like to sketch in Japan because "the Japanese do it so much better," but she thought all the figures of Buddha hideous. She found eucalyptus lozenges essential to her health in "unsanitary Tokyo." A visit to the Chinese Missionary Home in Shanghai thrilled her, but she was disappointed when "Happy Valley" in Hong Kong turned out to be a cemetery. She loved Australia, finding the "select tone of the people" to her liking, but detested one of her ship cabin mates there, "not a nice little baby, she squeaked so." Eager to be home, and quite satisfied with her successful adventures, she was sorry to end her diary with an unfortunate boat collision just outside Plymouth.

34

notice except the fact that he had put it into the train,
whereas if he had left it alone it would have been put in
with everyone else's, but, noticing his attentions, I then
tried to hand him a "tip" of 25 cents and dismiss him, but he
ignored my movements, so I watched to see what would happen.
Just as the train moved off he jumped on, and, when reaching
the Wharf, again took charge of my luggage. By this time I
saw through him. Then, having landed it safely, he demanded
2 dollars. "Well," thought I, "8/2d. for this!" I appealed
to the Chief Steward; a lot of jabbering then went on between
the fellow and the steward. They all talked to each other
in Spanish but understood one perfectly in English and always
replied in our tongue when <u>convenient</u>, I then asked the
steward whether he thought one dollar would satisfy the man
to which he acquiesced, and I then handed him an American paper
dollar, at which his face beamed and he went off saying "God
be with you ma'am", and I wondered what I had done, but felt
certain there was something wrong! I afterwards learned from
the Purser that in Panama the value of money is all half
American, one dollar is really 50 cents or worth our 2/0½d.
and 2 dollars is only 4/1d. But, being ignorant of this fact,
I had given the porter 4/1d. instead of 2/- which would have
satisfied him. Well, it's all an experience; I have enjoyed
laughing over it and no doubt he is still chuckling at his
own cleverness! I understand that many tourists are ignorant
of this fact regarding Panama money when first entering the
place, which explains why I had been warned of "fleecing".

35

There is really not much fleecing about it if they only knew
the value of money. For instance, an American lady told me
that the Tivoli Hotel charged 7 dollars a day or about 29/-,
and an American gentleman told me it cost 30/- per day - so
that I conclude neither of them knew that 7 dollars are really
only equal to about 14/-.

To return to my arrival on the Peru. I had scanned my
fellow travellers during the railway journey, and cannot say
that I am likely to bring any of them home with me! Such a
motley crew of 12; perhaps it is as well to be so few. I
certainly do not want more of the same order. There is a
woman whom I judge to be a cook by profession; I can only
picture her sitting in a kitchen between her labours with
her elbows lying across the table, as she sits now <u>hour after
hour,</u> in the Saloon a big, fat, black creature clothed in

a print garment of huge pat-
tern. She speaks to no-one
but grins benignly as one
passes her. I presume she
is Spanish. Then there is a
priest of very comely proportions, whose sole occupation
is eating and sprawling in a
hammock chair with his treble
chin resting on his cushioned
breast and his eyes closed in
blissful meditation.

"The Priest on S.S. Peru."

Charles Royce Barney

JULY 3, 1910

Charles Royce Barney donated his compact and pocket-worn Trip Log for 1909–1912 to the Sierra Club. This San Francisco resident took advantage of every opportunity to escape to the country by whatever means available—ferry, train, wagon, on foot—either alone or with comrades. His log captures both day outings and longer excursions and includes gear lists, expenses, and routes. The murky photographs that accompany his entries concentrate a view into wilderness that may no longer exist, amplifying particular times and places in a way that his prosaic writing does not. When every scene and experience is new, illustrations validate impressions and root them in depiction, lending strength to "the unwordable things that one wants to write about," as Canadian artist and diarist Emily Carr put it. No stranger to more remote destinations, Barney kept and donated a larger, second diary devoted to his trip through Kings Canyon in 1907.

"Lay and watched the shadows on Tehipite Dome a while as it slowly grew in definition like a photographic negative under the increasing light of the dawning day. The cracks and creases on its scarred face appeared one by one until the sun crowned it with a broad shaft of light while the canyon itself lay in deep shadow."

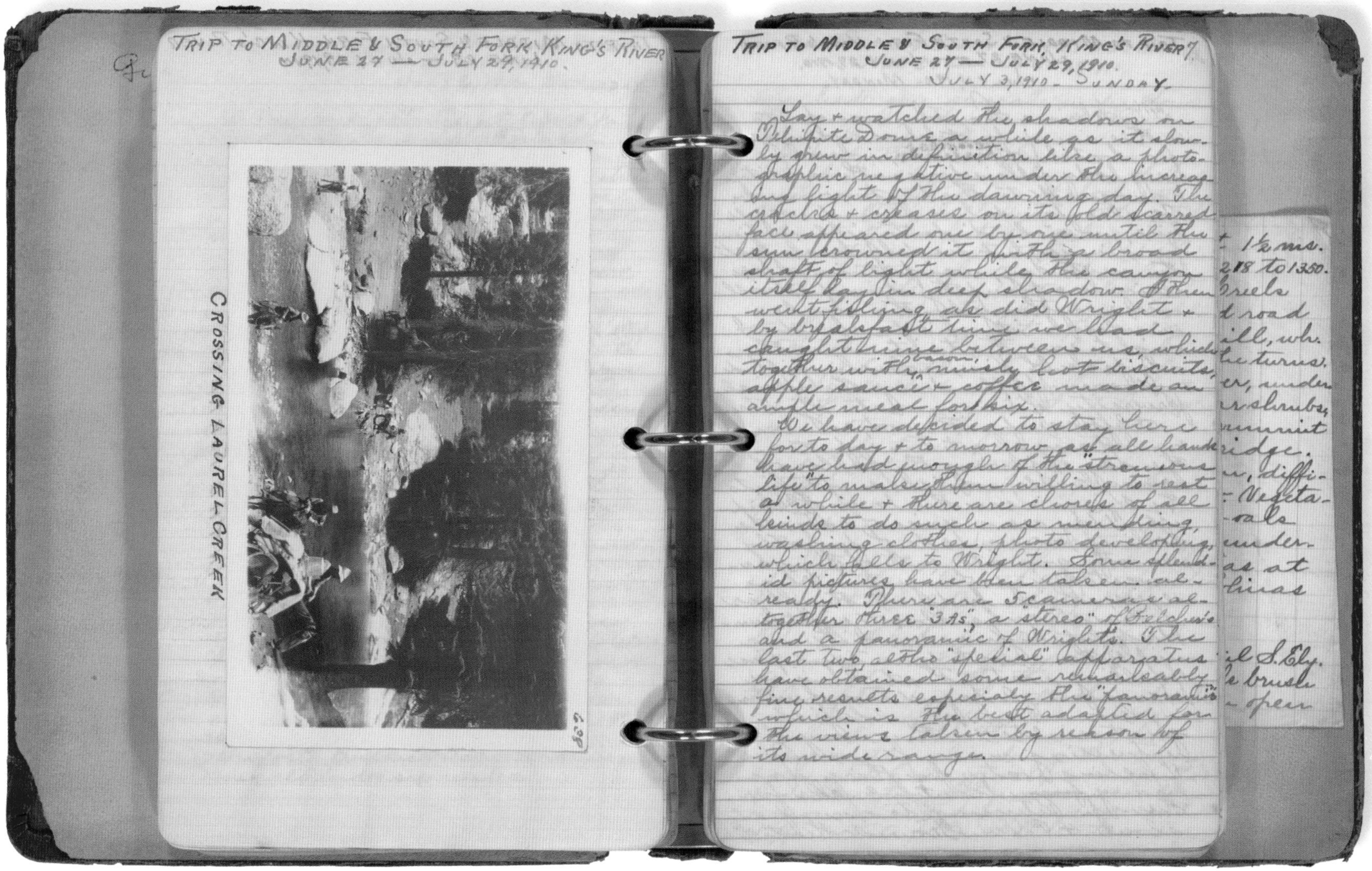

TRIP TO MIDDLE & SOUTH FORK KING'S RIVER
JUNE 27 — JULY 29, 1910.

CROSSING LAUREL CREEK

TRIP TO MIDDLE & SOUTH FORK, KING'S RIVER
JUNE 27 — JULY 29, 1910.

JULY 3, 1910 - SUNDAY.

Lay & watched the shadows on
Delhite Dome a while as it slowly grew in definition like a photographic negative under the increasing light of the dawning day. The
spectra & creases on its old scarred
face appeared one by one until the
sun crowned it with a broad
shaft of light while the canyon
itself lay in deep shadow. Then
went fishing as did Wright &
by breakfast time we had
caught nine between us which
together with nicely brown hot biscuits,
apple sauce & coffee made an
ample meal for six.

We have decided to stay here
for to day & to morrow as all hands
have had enough of the "strenuous
life to make them willing to rest
a while & there are chores of all
kinds to do such as mending,
washing clothes, photo developing,
which falls to Wright. Some splendid pictures have been taken already. There are 3 cameras altogether three "3½", a stereo" of Field's
and a panoramic of Wright's. The
last two, the "special" apparatus
have obtained some remarkably
fine results especialy the "panoramic"
which is the best adapted for
the views taken by reason of
its wide range.

[right margin partial text:]
+ 1½ ms.
218 to 1350.
reels
d road
ill, wh.
te turns.
er, under
r shrubs,
ummit
ridge.
e, diffi-
Vegeta-
als
under-
as at
lines

l S. Ely.
s brush
e open

William Otis Raiguel

AUGUST 23, 1911

Every one gave me a splendid reception but my French was so bad that I felt I was in the way and left and saw the town in the afternoon. See photos.

Architectural draftsman and office manager William Otis Raiguel kept diaries of his two trips to Europe that reflect his professional interests. The reader of these diaries witnesses Raiguel's ideas in the making as he draws and describes buildings and neighborhoods that he saw on his travels. His 1905 diary is small, tidy, and beautifully adorned with watercolors, but it is the diary from 1911, when he was thirty-six and newly married to Florence, that is pictured here. Traveling by train and ship from San Francisco to Canada, England, Scotland, Holland, Belgium, France, Switzerland, Austria, Italy, Greece, and Egypt, the couple sat in boulevard cafés, attended concerts, had luncheons with fellow expatriates, and wandered the streets remarking on the landscape and buildings. The rather ornery Raiguel frequently expressed his intolerance for others in his entries, but he was game enough to climb the Jungfrau by starlight with only a candle lantern. He worked with architect John Galen Howard on numerous San Francisco Bay Area buildings but moved away to an exclusive residential section of Monterey in 1926. Considered by the trade to be "of a more or less eccentric nature," Raiguel later took his own life after shooting his dog and possibly Florence as well, though this was never proved.

Courtesy of the Environmental Design Archives, University of California, Berkeley

"I ordered the donkey to stop and I went in to investigate."

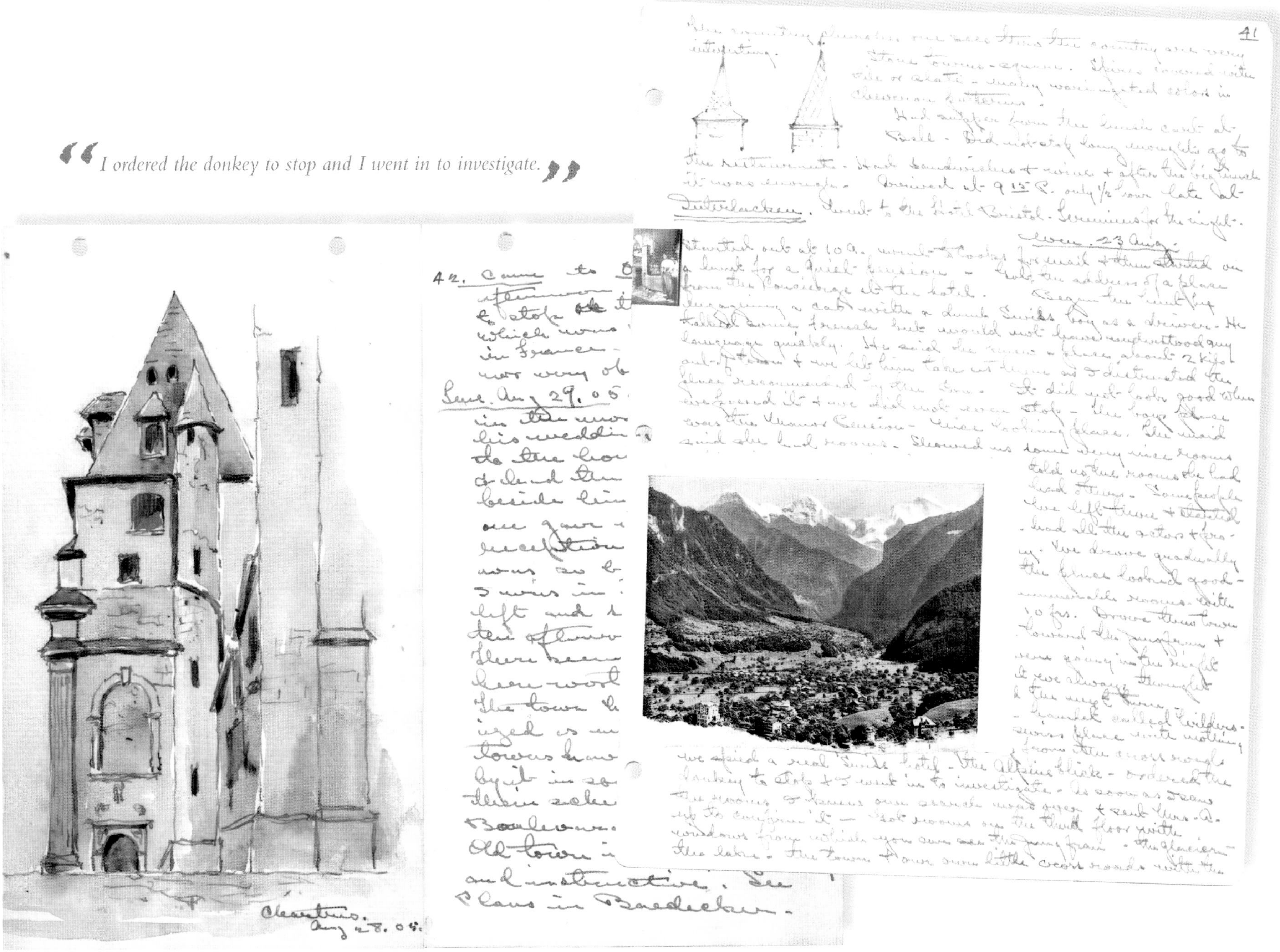

Constance M. Topping

NOVEMBER 15, 1915–APRIL 20, 1916

Constance Topping began keeping her "Diaries of Dippydom," "Records of Rats-on-the-Roof," and "Categories of Crazy Connie" when she was thirteen and continued them until she was thirty and a teacher of English at her alma mater, Berkeley High School. She recorded in her private volumes all the thrills, aspirations, and disappointments of a young woman. "If inside this book you spy, your fate is,—well,—oh me, oh my." Crazy about the boys and the dances when she was sixteen, Constance noted in her diary the days on which she'd received a smile from her certain someone, and the days she didn't, which brought on "a blubbering spell." She included updates on the war, confetti, favorite phrases, card and gift lists, names of boys she admired, caricatures of her teachers, and long columns of all the books she'd read during the year. She didn't guess she liked teas much. She wrote poetry in her journals, later becoming a poet "on the outermost fringe of the local group of writers," as she described herself in a letter to Dane Coolidge in 1936. The Constance Topping Memorial Poetry Prize, established in 1927, is still awarded today at the Berkeley Poets' Dinner.

❖ Canadian artist Emily Carr wrote, "I used to write diaries when I was young, but if I put anything down that was under the skin I was in terror that someone would read it and ridicule me, so I always burnt them up before long.…I wonder why we are always ashamed of our best parts and try to hide them." Though teenage diaries are usually destroyed in cringing mortification once those melodramatic years have been left behind, Topping did the world a favor and preserved hers from the incinerator. ❖ The initials "P. W." on this page represent Philip Wood, a flame of hers who was called away to the Great War.

MEMBERS OF THE CLASS OF 1921,
THE BLUE AND GOLD, VOL. 47,
UNIVERSITY ARCHIVES.

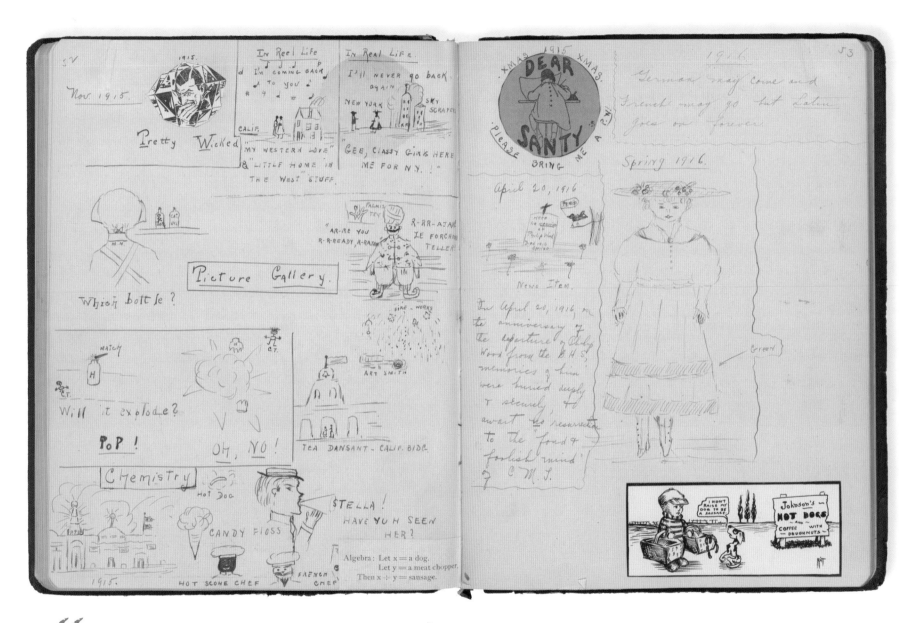

> *Harold is just as nice as can be to me, but he seems to like Leonore, Hester, Hazel or anyone better than me. He talks politics and automobiles to me and laughs with them. Kenneth Graham is going to get canned from German if he isn't careful. Why do I like "no-accounts?"*

Florence Merriam Bailey

JULY 26, 1917

Bits of plant fluff, grass stalks, a lock of mountain sheep hair jubilantly found in a crack in the rock face she was climbing, fern fronds, and feathers of all sorts illustrate the many field diaries of Florence Merriam Bailey. Secured with safety pins, rusty paper clips, or incisions in the page, these bits of the natural world accompany minute and very personal accounts of her surroundings. Portrayals of the interwoven patterns of light, plant, sound, creature, and rock around her constitute the entries on her signature blue pages. The color, movement, and reflection of light, in particular, stir her to luminous expression. ❖ Entering Glacier National Park on July 4 in the war year of 1917, Bailey remarks on the abundance of uniforms and revelry, and the liquor sold in "aggressively open towns in a wet state." She also expresses dismay at the "tawdry decoration" in the park—the totem poles, Japanese lanterns, Indians dressed in blankets who must pose for photographs for a dime, and waitresses in Alpine costume. ❖ An ornithologist married to a mammalogist whose primary residence was in Washington DC, Bailey spent long periods of time hiking, climbing, and camping in remote areas with her husband, "Mr. Bailey" or "The Scientist," observing and recording scat, sign, tracks, and renditions of birdsong. She took grizzly prints with candle wax and recognized a lazuli bunting "by the burr in its song." While at home, she established the Washington DC Audubon Society and became the first female associate member of the

FLORENCE MERRIAM BAILEY, DONNER PEAK CAMP, JULY 1900, WILDLIFE, PLANTS, INDIANS, AND WESTERN SCENES FROM THE VERNON BAILEY COLLECTION.

Ornithologists Union in 1885. At the forefront of the movement to use binoculars rather than shotguns to observe birds, she imbued her field notes with warmth, personality, and a side commentary that make them far more than dry scientific documents. As Thoreau wrote, she "listened for the literary overtones of the distant call of the loon." She truly exulted in each day, and her joy in observation is manifest. ❖ "Piegan Camp" was one of the many stops during the Baileys' two-month exploration of Glacier National Park.

> ❝ *One big stretch of yellow dog-tooth violets made the central rug of our floor, but other colors along the borders delighted the eye. As soon as the horses were unsaddled they had to be quickly driven out of camp before they rolled on the flowers.* ❞

RUSSELL RAY DOLLARHIDE, SIGNAL CORPS,
"CAMP LEWIS, WASHINGTON, ROOKIE DAYS,
1917–1918," RUSSELL RAY DOLLARHIDE
WORLD WAR I PHOTOGRAPH ALBUM.

Russell Ray Dollarhide

MARCH 23, 1918

His girlfriend Julia sent Russell Dollarhide a blank "Soldier's Diary" (English-French edition) shortly after he began his basic training at Camp Lewis in Washington State. It arrived with its companion volume, *The Soldier's French Phrase Book.* It is clear that Dollarhide took both filling the pages of his diary and studying his phrasebook seriously, though he was frequently bored, writing "Every day the same, nothing to write about." "A buck private in the rear rank" of the Signal Corps, he spent his time on hikes, motorcycle practice, tear gas trials, and building field kitchens, latrines, and incinerators. He volunteered to work in his battalion's tailor shop in order to get relief from KP duty. When they boarded a train for East Coast deployment to Europe, the towns along the tracks either ignored the soldiers or turned out to cheer, plying the men with cookies, doughnuts, cigarettes, magazines, and candy apples. In New York Dollarhide endlessly washed windows and experienced bunk fatigue when he was quarantined with measles, but he was finally cleared for passage. "The inspection consisted of holding up an extra pair of pants and shoes, so guess if you have a pair of pants and shoes, you can go to France." Throughout the diary, his witty cartoon illustrations belie the worry and seriousness of his situation. His last entry, on May 9, 1918, reads, "This finishes this book and also our stay in the USA. Next installment will be published abroad. Bon voyage."

A **Soldier's Diary**
Date_____

Mar 23 Continued.
came over here to write a
letter to Julia but it's late,
I'm sleepy, can't think of
any thing to write so guess
I will go over and crawl
in the hay. It sure is raining.
The dashing boys who are
light on their feet are
giving a dance tonight up
at the K.C. hall. The fine
company at Tacoma is
furnishing the "girls."
Understand we can't keep
a dairy in France so guess
I had better fill this up
and send it to you. Will

A **Soldier's Diary**
Date_____

probably be so that I
can fill up several more
before we leave here.

There goes The Call for reveille
I love To hear iT Summon Me —
I love To Get up iN The MorNiNg To
I Do I Do — Like hell I Do.

❝...understand we can't keep a diary in France so guess I had better fill this up and send it to you. ❞

Bob Marshall

JULY 7, 1919

Bob Marshall began his short life of dedicated forestry and wilderness and social activism while still a boy. By the age of fifteen he had already started compiling his Adirondack Notebooks, field diaries of measurements, careful observation, and reporting while on walks, camping trips, and climbing expeditions with his younger brother and best friend, George, in the wild places of northern New York. He named the walks for things encountered on the routes: Sheep Skull Walk, Galloping Doe Walk. Routes were very important to Marshall, and he liked repeating the same courses in different seasons to see what had changed. He loved taking the family canoe as far up the creek past the beaver dam as it could go, tramping barefoot through mud and marshes, passing through untrammeled places. Even in pouring rain, he and George would set out through the front gate—"We'd made up our minds to go, so we went." Marshall dependably described plants and birds, but he and George also succumbed to youthful exuberance and mischief, tunneling into sand banks, keeping a tennis ball continually bouncing between them as they walked, and hiding to avoid railroad agents, who could evict them from the railroad lands on which they were trespassing to pick wild berries. On one long walk when Bob was "5/6 a man," George caught a ride home with a neighbor, but Bob preferred to run all the way and arrived in the yard at the same time, "in plenty of time for supper." ❧ Meticulous and critical, Marshall wrote diary entries that seem like practice exercises for what he would become.

ROBERT MARSHALL, WRIGHT PEAK, ADIRONDACKS, SEPTEMBER 1921, PHOTOGRAPHS FROM THE ROBERT MARSHALL PAPERS.

They portend the undaunted spirit and the belief that wilderness is a social as well as environmental necessity that would take him far afield, to Montana and Alaska. In 1933 he expanded on the style of his early diaries when he documented his fifteen-month sojourn in Wiseman, Alaska, resulting in his book *Arctic Village*. Credited with the founding in 1935 of The Wilderness Society, the first organization dedicated to wilderness preservation, Marshall also continued his support for civil rights and fair labor initiatives until his sudden death at the age of thirty-eight in 1939.

MILL ON THE FLUSS
AND VICINITY

The Mill on the Fluss.   10-16

The Roadside
About a quarter of a mile below the
Mill on the Fluss

Lake, Green Outlet   5-14
From bridge just below the Mill

When the I live I saw   8-15
From Mill Road. Back of the flow the cleared fields
of Forest Home can plainly be seen on the side of
Forest Home Mountain

> *It was very cold crossing the meadow; the west wind blowing the rain through the fifty degree Fahrenheit air into our faces. All thru Forest Home I refused to put my hands in my pockets, tho they were quite cold, telling George that I did not wish to create a bad impression. However, the only signs of life we saw were a boy and two dogs.*

Charles W. Seffens

AUGUST 25–AUGUST 26, 1925

> "In the early afternoon Dad and Margaret drove up to the hotel and from there took a walk of about three-quarters of a mile to the "Boiling Lake." It was quite hilly and pretty warm and we took it slow and easy. Margaret stood the "hike" fine and was very proud of her achievement."

An increase in the number of trip diaries, such as the Seffens family's "In the Good Old Summertime," followed the surge of automobile touring that began around the time of the Panama-Pacific International Exposition in San Francisco in 1915, when intrepid Easterners headed west for recreation, taking in the new national parks along the way. Advances in photography, relative prosperity, and increased services for auto travelers meant that the journeys were a bit less daunting than in the past, though still worthy of eloquent documentation. ❖ The five members of the Seffens family set out in the summer of 1925 from their home in Newburg, California, in a 1921 Studebaker on a fifteen-day, eleven-hundred-mile, eighty-six-gallons-of-gasoline (no oil) tour of eleven neighboring counties, camping and visiting natural wonders, construction projects, friends, and county seats along the way. While they traveled with "all the comforts of home packed tidily into the car—everything folds!"—they frequently met with car trouble and impassable roads. The travelers encountered help in the form of new friends and memorable experiences, which all contributed to the adventure that concluded when they pulled into their driveway at home. The satisfied postscript: "Humboldt is a good place to live in."

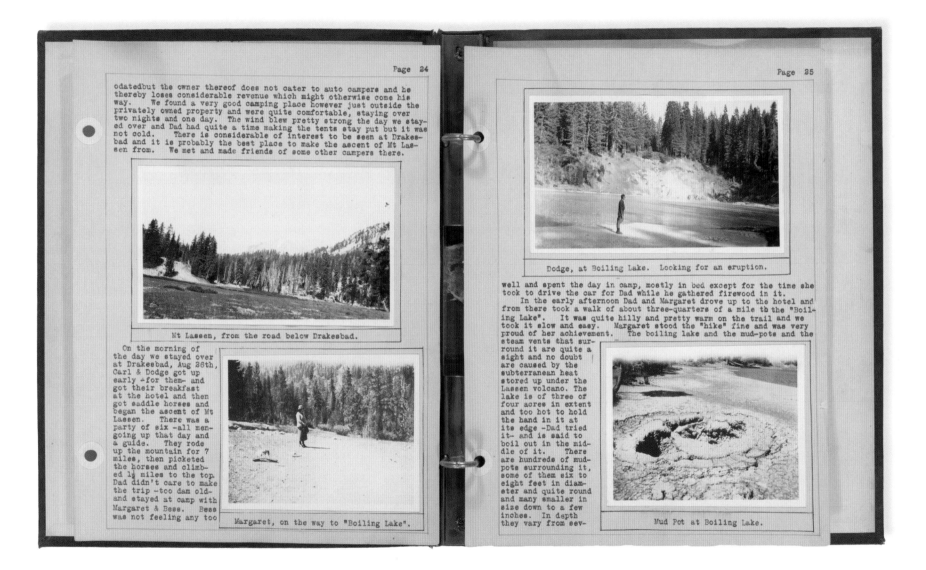

Page 24

odatedbut the owner thereof does not cater to auto campers and he thereby loses considerable revenue which might otherwise come his way.   We found a very good camping place however just outside the privately owned property and were quite comfortable, staying over two nights and one day. The wind blew pretty strong the day we stayed over and Dad had quite a time making the tents stay put but it was not cold.   There is considerable of interest to be seen at Drakesbad and it is probably the best place to make the ascent of Mt Lassen from.   We met and made friends of some other campers there.

Mt Lassen, from the road below Drakesbad.

On the morning of the day we stayed over at Drakesbad, Aug 26th, Carl & Dodge got up early –for them– and got their breakfast at the hotel and then got saddle horses and began the ascent of Mt Lassen.   There was a party of six –all men– going up that day and a guide.   They rode up the mountain for 7 miles, then picketed the horses and climbed 1½ miles to the top. Dad didn't care to make the trip –too dam old– and stayed at camp with Margaret & Bess.   Bess was not feeling any too

Margaret, on the way to "Boiling Lake".

Page 25

Dodge, at Boiling Lake. Looking for an eruption.

well and spent the day in camp, mostly in bed except for the time she took to drive the car for Dad while he gathered firewood in it.
In the early afternoon Dad and Margaret drove up to the hotel and from there took a walk of about three-quarters of a mile tb the "Boiling Lake".   It was quite hilly and pretty warm on the trail and we took it slow and easy.   Margaret stood the "hike" fine and was very proud of her achievement.   The boiling lake and the mud-pots and the steam vents that surround it are quite a sight and no doubt are caused by the subterranean heat stored up under the Lassen volcano. The lake is of three of four acres in extent and too hot to hold the hand in it at its edge –Dad tried it– and is said to boil out in the middle of it.   There are hundreds of mud-pots surrounding it, some of them six to eight feet in diameter and quite round and many smaller in size down to a few inches. In depth they vary from sev-

Mud Pot at Boiling Lake.

In one place there is an area of about forty feet square which is given entirely over to escaping steam, which every minute or two "shoots" like the safety valve of a steam engine. It is very wonderful to see and there is a strong smell of sulphur in the air.

Mrs. Minnie Perrelet, Miss Mary Muth, Mr. Charles Puck

JANUARY 12, 1926

A communal diary illustrated with photographs, or a heavily captioned photograph album? The introduction to "Death Valley Trip" reads, "This trip started at 3rd and Central Ave. Los Angeles Calif. Jan. 8, 1926 at 4:10 pm…" There were six people in three cars—a Ford Touring, a Ford Roadster known as the Grubwagon, and a Star. The nine-day minimalist excursion into the desert, which had yet to offer paved roads, roadside cafés, and other welcoming amenities to tourists, did nothing to diminish the high spirits and evident joy of this gumptious group.

Mr. A. E. Dimock, Mr. Guy Billyon, Mr. George Abbott

double road
for
...
...o down
...a hundred
...clutch
...we
...picture

On the Way to Rhyolite

❝*We arrive at Confidence Mills, a very aged mining venture. The driver of the grub wagon upon spying the cog wheel decided it would be just the thing for his ranch but when he came to pick it up decided for his flivver's sake to leave it.*❞

Sanders Russell

MARCH 12–MARCH 15, 1926

A seldom still, curious, creative, and mischievous boy who kept diaries from the age of nine, Sanders Russell was born in 1913 and raised by an adoring mother in Glendale, California. His small datebook-type journals tell of many visits to the movies, sometimes at the Hollywood Bowl, rows with his teachers, maintaining the school track, swimming in the river, and playing games of cops and robbers, mahjong, marbles, real estate, and baseball in vacant lots. He made a breadboard for his mother, chloroformed his cat, and fell through a neighbor's roof. He continually sent away for things— free toothpaste, coins—and collected bottle tops and cigar bands. Later, Russell won some repute as a poet and coedited the *Experimental Review* in 1940 with his longtime friend Robert Duncan. Critic Donald Merriam Allen wrote that Russell's work "realized…an immediate correspondence between inner being and outer world." Sanders Russell's childhood diaries shelter the spark of the future poet.

> **"** *Got 3 rare bottle tops from Buddy for $30. Got some loquats. Played in vacant house next to Duncan's. Got some poison oak on me.* **"**

SANDERS RUSSELL, "SANDY, 10½, GOLF MAN," SANDERS RUSSELL PHOTOGRAPH COLLECTION.

Ina Sizer Cassidy and Gerald Cassidy

JULY 21, 1926

Ira Cassidy changed his name to Gerald when he moved from New York, where he was employed as a draftsman and commercial poster artist, to Santa Fe, New Mexico, in 1912 in order to save his failing health. At the same time he married Perlina (Ina) Sizer, a women's rights crusader who had grown up in a log cabin in Colorado. Gerald began to paint and Ina to write, and they became accomplished and beloved members of the artistic community of the Southwest, partisans of the Navajo, and an inseparable couple. In 1926, with financial assistance from one of Gerald's patrons, they embarked for a year in Europe, renting a studio in Paris and visiting the great galleries and art centers in hopes of securing an exhibition and a gallery. "Gerald is launched in the art world of Paris!" During the course of their stay, Ina wrote in dense, typewritten pages wide-ranging descriptions of their days, covering politics, religion, education, and the infrastructure of the places they visited—France, England, Italy, and Tunisia. Both Gerald and Ina contributed drawings to the collaborative journal—drawings of people they met, flora, and buildings. Ina wrote, "I did not know what gorgeous colors were in the sea until now," and they both tried to capture those in words and pictures.

> *He advised us to remain away from crowds, just as every one has since we have been here. We are so impressed with the advice that we never get near any crowd, even to see a dog fight, or hear the street singers who are so numerous here.*

GERALD AND INA CASSIDY, BANCROFT PORTRAIT COLLECTION.

Paris. Atelier 19,50 rue Vercingetorix.
July 21st, Wednesday.

Bettie Young surprised me this morning by walking in on me. I did not know where she was, as she had left about three weeks ago for an automobile trip through the south of France. She has been at Carcasonne to see the burning of the city, which she says was a marvelous spectacle. It was in celebration of the destruction of the city by some body or other, way back in the dim distant past.

Any way, Bettie came, and wanted me to go shopping with her, as it is so hot in the south of France where they have been motoring that she cannot wear comfortably any clothes she has. So we went to Paul Poirets. It is always a joy to go there on any p retext. Their things are so very lovely and distinctive. They had very little on hand and nothing that Betty liked. But we found that all of their prices had been raised above what they were when we went in May, and on top of this raise they add 25 per cent in order to keep up with the falling franc. It is 49.20 this morning, lower than at any time since we have been here. When we first came it was about 27 to the dollar. We have seen it go down, down until now it is almost fifty, or two cents where it should be ,if at normal, about 20 cents.

From Poirets we went to Lanvin's, with no better luck. I had not been in this establishment before, and while it is distinctive, it does no approach Poiret's. She is supposed to be very smart, however. At Poiret's they go in for embellishments in the way of wool embroidery and now it is handpainted dresses, especially the use of the same sort of brilliant, sparkling paints that are used for brilliant(and generally guady) lampshades, but it doesnt look 'guady' on Poiret's things, for he knows how to combine colors.

Then we went to Recamier's for luncheon, where Gerald met us, as we had left a xx not at the studio for him, he being at the Academy. And Bettie told us about the trouble she had been having with her new car, and how she was stalled near Carcasonne waiting for parts, and had been obliged to come up to Paris for them, as well as for some thin clothes.They are having a splendid time.

After luncheon we went to Morgan Harjes for the mail, and to get some money. It x was here that Betty urged us to be very careful in Paris, on account of the falling exchange, as there is no way of telling what the French may do. Two cabinets have fallen and the third is just formed, yet tottering. This Cabinet is a Socialist one, and doesnt seem to have the confidence of the people. We said that we didnt think there was any danger, but she insists that we cant tell. This is the way the French Revolutio started, all of sudden after so much muttering. She reminded us that we were living in the very section of Paris in which trouble would first come, among the working class.

It seems far fetched to fear anything. But Bettie made us promise that if any trouble should arise we would immediately 'beat it' to some place outside of Paris, and to keep plenty of money on hand for any emergency. It really sounded foolish. But thinking it could do no harm in any event, I went in to see the banker, and had a long talk with him. He said he didnt think there would be any trouble, but acknowledged that there was no way of telling before hand what the people might do, and told of an assault last night in the Montmarte district upon an American. I had not seen it in the Herald, and he said it had not appeared in any of the English papers, but had been in the French papers. He said it was a case, he thought, of a foolish tourist, perhaps with a few drinks, who had no understanding of the temper of the French, and had made a remark which they took exception to. But no damage had been done. But it shows what might happen. He advised us to remain away from crowds, just as every one has since we have been here. We are so impressed with the advice that we never get near any crowd, even to see a dog fight, or hear the street singers who are so numerous here.

This evening's papers record the fall of the new Socialist Cabinet, after a strong vote of 'no confidence', and less than 60 million francs in the treasury!

What the outcome is to be no one can predict. We are assured that it is all political. The politicians and the speculators do not want a staple money, so they are doing all they can to prevent stabilization of the franc, and stir up as much hatred among the people against America on account of the war debts, as it is possible to do, in order to keep the people from thinking the politicians are to blame for the financial conditions at the present moment. What the outcome will be no one knows. But in the meantime, we are working along with both eyes and ears open, for whatever may happen. We may be forced to leave.

David Ross Brower

MAY 24, 1928; FEBRUARY 7, 1931

When he was fifteen, David Brower kept three volumes of "Butterfly Captures and Weather Record," in which he recorded a daily weather report and his forays into the wild areas adjacent to Berkeley, California, in search of butterflies. These were the first of many journals he would keep. Most weekends and many afternoons, he ranged across the East Bay hills, alone or with friends or his mother, on foot or bicycle, gathering figwort to feed his caterpillars, "stalking scenes" with his Kodak, naming clouds, and describing the flight patterns and behavior of butterflies. Sometimes he missed catches because he was too busy observing the butterfly and so forgot to net it. A particular challenge he faced was keeping the long handle of his butterfly net out of his bicycle spokes while riding. At the age of eighteen, Brower was already taking extensive hiking trips into the Sierra Nevada, to places he would later champion as director of the Sierra Club, Friends of the Earth, and Earth Island Institute. Riding and sleeping in his buddy Ralph's "cranky car," eating cold tamales and canned sardines in deep snow, sledding down slopes on trashcan lids, Brower and his friends, "needing a little drive in college work," hiked many miles throughout

DAVID BROWER, 1934, DAVID ROSS BROWER PHOTOGRAPH COLLECTION

Yosemite Valley in 1931. Still observing weather patterns, he wrote, "Sierra weather is a puzzle to me." ❧ A groundbreaking climber, Brower made seventy first ascents and led many thousands of people into remote areas over the course of his lifetime. His early journals point to the wilderness activist he would become, but they also show a meticulous, fun-loving, and hungry young man. When he was nineteen he wrote, "No one interested in nature at all can reach a state where there isn't something novel in Yosemite. We are all ready to go again. All we need is a car and finances," and "My one hope for a future lies in keeping above the benumbing state of monotony which has gotten into the rest of the 'business' world, and I certainly figure a summer in the Sierras furthers that end."

> **"** *I took my second trip of the week into the Hills. I like the map Idea, and I think I'll try it again.* **"**

12 From now on, don't stop at the half way mark. **13**

there long ago. It is a film fault, and should be ignored. I let the camera rest for a while then, knowing that I should save films for the better pictures above. I considered I was "above" when I got this view of Sentinel Rock, and a snow covered "zig" or two in the foreground, covered with snow and ice. This picture, too, was unfortunately light-struck. The altitude and snow increased together. As soon as we got into a N.E. ravine we got into the thick of it, and will be there for several pages. This picture shows the ravine. The trail is to be seen ahead in the upper part of the picture and under the "Sentinel" picture. Geo. with his Daniel Boone hat and Vernon with a shovel he inadvertently picked up below grace the picture, too.

Before we reached Glacier Point the depth of the snow made walking laborious. Our feet sank in from six to ten inches on all but the well packed snow on the trail, and that was packed so hard it had be—

Trail snaps

Short Trail
Yos. Nat. Park.

> "A dozen eggs, 2 quarts of chocolate and a half pound of bacon furnished our meager breakfast. We ate so much that George suggested that we climb the first little step of the falls there."

Abner Doble

AUGUST 16–AUGUST 17, 1931

Legendary engineer and visionary Abner Doble was an inveterate list maker. His twenty-three years' worth of daily to-do lists make a stunning demonstration of how much character and life these lists can reveal. He compiled them from 1910, at the age of twenty, until 1933 in uniform, sturdy, red volumes sold commercially as The National Diary. Very rarely is there an item on his list that does not have a corresponding checkmark beside it to show that the task or thought or topic for discussion was completed. Some list items spawned sublists, and some were calculations, memos, or photographs. "Order cig (Turkish) and benzine [for lighter]; make Buckan foreman; blow steel today; see about dog; why not 4:1 gear ratio?; send Mrs. Taylor a Drip-O-Lator; bring paste home; specs for crank-pin-bearing; write to Evans to try a standard separator on bus 607; get carpenter to bind up firewood; chiropodist at 12:30; get chair fixed; it would be nice if Sticky were offered a job; install Iron Fireman in shop boiler; celebration of 6th anniversary—bottle of champagne; lunch with Charley Fisher (this man has proved himself to be spineless and without integrity or vision); get toaster plug changed; office button code: one, come downstairs; two, tea; three, lad wanted; 3 cyl. triple built like 2cc engine; phone mother; sail for New Zealand on 'Monowai.'" One poignant entry is a note that his ten-year-old son, Abner, had died from falling off the roof. On his list for November 23, 1931: "Buy two more of these diaries."

❖ The daily lists create a picture of Doble's life no less vivid than a

"Abner Doble in the driver's seat,"
Doble Steam Motors Corporation
photograph collection.

Sunday, August 16, 1931

✓ 1. Bill Doble's birthday.

✓ 2. Write Warren: See page 27-7-31.

   ✗ a. Were dripolators & tires sent to N.Z.?

   ✓ b. Besler's letters. ✗ Give Warren the facts.

✓ 3. Rear Axle for Lorry: Our present design is unduly complicated and expensive.

a. Axle-forging with integral-flange

b. Cap "A" in halves, holds bearing in place.

c. Bearing "B" in one piece; contains roller-bearing, brake-spider and spring-seat: lined with phos. Bronze.

d. Hard steel bushing pressed onto axle-tube and screwed to flange.

e. Axle forging runs right up to roller-bearing to reduce pry, and relieved in center and holds oil.

f. Cast large oil pocket in spring saddle.

g. Install dust guard in cap "A".

h. Perhaps bushings can be short and at each end only.

Monday, August 17, 1931

✓ 1. Pay radio tax.

✓ 2. Show Mr. Hutt axle design. [Send to Mr. Alley.]

✓ 3. Check boiler coils for heating-surface, and gas-passage-area, etc.

✓ 4. Write N.Z. and send latest prints.

✓ 5. Collect expenses of £10.0.0 (OK Mr. Alley)

✓ 6. Write Frank Bell:—

   ✓ a. Use cyl. cover on top-end of aux. engine.

   ✓ b. Could increase counterweight radius and

   ✓ c. Use narrower diff. bearing: thicker counterweight

✓ 7. Axle shaft, for stress of 12,500#/sq. in.
4¼" dia shaft: 143,000 lb in torsion and 11,000#" bending. From Fig 3 page 1570 Kent = 3.95 approx. Say 4" dia.

   a. For hollow shaft with hole ½ O.D. then $O.D. = d \div (\sqrt[3]{1 - \text{ratio } OD \text{ to } ID})$ or $O.D. = 4 \div (\sqrt[3]{½} \quad ; = 4 \div .795 = 5.05"\text{ dia}?$

   b. Assume 4¼" shaft. With 2⅛" hole will weigh ¾, and have 93.75% of strength.

✓ 8. See Real Estate Agent.

✓ 9. Put rear springs below-axle.

✓ 10. Get "Invitation to the Waltz" Phil. Sym. Orch.

✓ 11. Engine (NZ "H"): Why crank-pin-cap?

   a. Perhaps pin could be so

   b. Wrist-pin thinner and longer tapers

✓ 12. Make a thorough study of N.Z. engine, to improve Sentinel-Engine.

narrative. Heirs to an engineering San Francisco family that made miners' tools and water wheels during the Gold Rush, Doble and his three younger brothers built their first steam car in their parents' basement while still in school. His brother Warren said that Abner would never stand for second-best, a drive for perfection that ultimately rendered their cars too expensive for commercial viability, but that also kept him insistent to the end of his days that steam was an option at least equal to gasoline. Abner started the diary pictured here after the Emeryville company he founded with his brothers, Doble Steam Motors, had declared bankruptcy, and while he was working as a consultant on steam engines around the world, including a steam bus in Auckland. ❧ Driving a Doble, it was said, was like riding on a magic carpet. There are many people today who read Doble's journals in their own pursuit of clean, quiet, cheap steam car technology. These volumes demonstrate handsomely that keepers of journals often use them as a way to search for solutions, not to dwell on problems.

"'ANTELOPE' ABNER DOBLE DRIVING, SPRING OF 1917," DOBLE STEAM MOTORS CORPORATION PHOTOGRAPH COLLECTION.

"Oil & water separated out of exhaust steam should be pumped at once into steam-line. Thus saving oil and eliminating cleaning bother! I think so!"

William Norris Dakin

OCTOBER 25–OCTOBER 26, 1936

"From artist to ore-buyer," Will Dakin faced an exciting challenge when called away from his job search after graduating from the San Francisco Art Institute during the Great Depression in 1934. His father worked as a mining engineer for the Texas Mining and Smelting Company in Sonora, Mexico, searching for antimony to support a growing war market, and he wanted his son to come south to assist him. Will began his narrative journal on Christmas Day, 1935, when he received the life-altering telegram from his father, and continued it until his return home almost two years later. His vividly graphic entries, made while traveling throughout Sonora, camping out in the desert, and working alongside people of diverse backgrounds, are accompanied in quantity by both rough black-and-white sketches and polished drawings in colored pencil. He had a fondness for portraying the working burros, miners, and residents in the pastoral countryside and busy towns, but it seems that his favorite subjects were the musicians he met in small, dark, and crowded rooms. Any free time he had was spent at the fiestas, bars, and homes from which the music called to him, his journal always at hand. Readers of these journals truly walk through the Sonoran landscape in his shoes. ❧ Later making his way as an artist with Disney Studios and the Eimac Corporation, Will Dakin wrote and drew in 194 diaries until his death in 1992, chronicling his life over the course of sixty years.

> *In the U.S., little boys play "cops and robbers." In Mexico they play "musicos," waving sticks for instruments. This morning I observed four of them outside the Ortega house, playing away on their imaginary contrabajos and trompetas.*

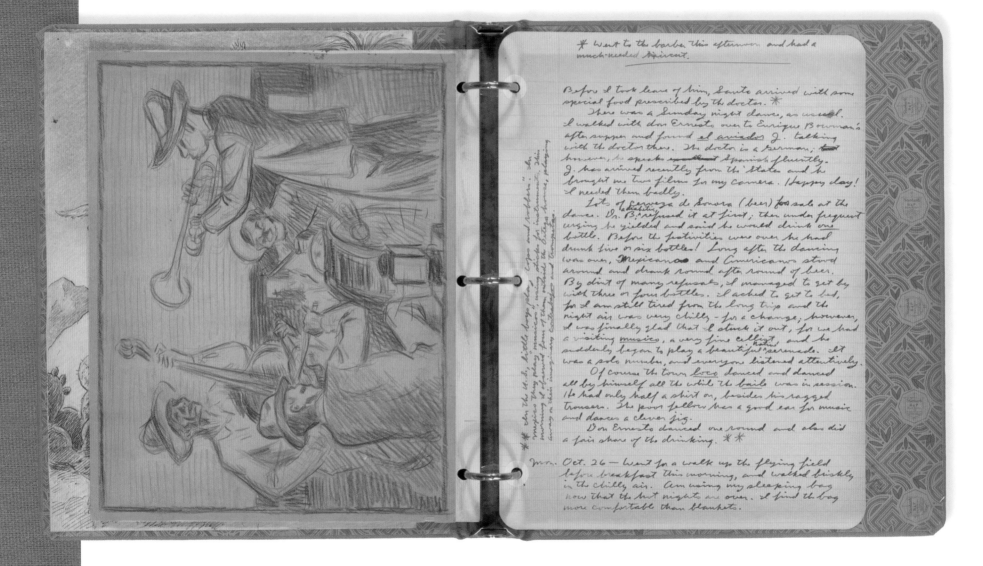

✳ Went to the barber this afternoon and had a much-needed haircut.

Before I took leave of him, Santo arrived with some special food prescribed by the doctor. ✳

There was a Sunday night dance, as usual. I walked with don Ernesto over to Enrique Bowman's after supper and found el aviador J. talking with the doctor there. The doctor is a German; however, he speaks Spanish fluently. J. has arrived recently from the 'States and he brought me two films for my camera. Happy day! I needed them badly.

Lots of Cerveza de Sonora (beer) for sale at the dance. Dr. B. refused it at first, then under frequent urging he yielded and said he would drink one bottle. Before the festivities were over he had drunk five or six bottles! Long after the dancing was over, Mexicans and Americans stood around and drank round after round of beer. By dint of many refusals, I managed to get by with three or four bottles. I ached to get to bed, for I am still tired from the long trip and the night air was very chilly – for a change; however, I was finally glad that I stuck it out, for we had a visiting músico, a very fine cellist, and he suddenly began to play a beautiful serenade. It was a solo number, and everyone listened attentively.

Of course the town loco danced and danced all by himself all the while the baile was in session. He had only half a shirt on, besides his ragged trousers. The poor fellow has a good ear for music and dances a clever jig.

Don Ernesto danced one round and also did a fair share of the drinking. ✳✳

Mon. Oct. 26 — Went for a walk up the flying field before breakfast this morning, and walked briskly in the chilly air. Am using my sleeping bag now that the hot nights are over. I find the bag more comfortable than blankets.

Yoshiko Uchida

JANUARY 9–JANUARY 11, 1943

When she was nine and ten years old, Yoshiko Uchida kept diaries recording the adoption and early deaths of her two puppies, Frisky and Brownie. Each diary ends with a colorful and tender memorial page resembling a decorated altar for her beloved pet. At the same time, she was writing stories with titles such as "Willie the Squirrel" and "Jimmy Chipmunk and His Friends." Her subsequent years were compiled in a three-ring binder until 1942, when she graduated from the University of California at Berkeley. These pages record a cheerful, busy, and innocent time of travel, events, friends, dates, fundraising bake sales, football games, and birthday parties. Nearly all entries are decorated with small cartoon-like drawings at the top or in the margins. In 1942, before she could receive her diploma, Uchida's world was turned upside down when her father was arrested by the FBI and she, her mother, and sister Kay received the order to vacate their home in Berkeley and join other Japanese Americans in the horse stalls of the Tanforan Racetrack for internment during World War II. Nine months later, the family was moved to the Topaz Relocation Camp in the Utah desert and reunited with her father, Dwight. Uchida taught third grade in the camp and tried to keep up her spirits, though she pined for "a just and lasting peace." Her father, who had always been active in his community, continued to be an activist and community leader in the camps,

"Family, Topaz, 1943," Yoshiko Uchida photograph collection.

"The F.B.I. are here again—questioning all those who signed Repatriation papers—what rats!!!"

"TOPAZ, UTAH, 1/10/43," YOSHIKO UCHIDA PAPERS.

and the family outspokenly protested beatings and unprovoked shootings by their MP guards, the paltry food allowance of 39 cents per day, and the practice of enlisting young Nisei men out of the camps "to be cannon fodder overseas." ❖ One can read in Uchida's diary her attempts to be positive and to help her young pupils with their confusion, sadness, and anxiety. Still, her writing and drawings also display an indomitable spirit as she calls their miserable barracks corner "our boudoir" and attempts to help others beset by the pernicious illnesses of the prison camps. Sober entries— "There is so much sadness in the world"—are innocently punctuated by "tsk-tsk," "whew," "lucky bum," "ugh," "poor fella," and many exclamation marks. She exults over a "precious single daffodil amid the black of tar paper and the beige of sand and dust," and "a whole flock of seagulls." She must have shared the sentiment of Anaïs Nin, "In my journal, I am at ease." ❖ Uchida eventually used her experiences at Topaz to write her novel *Journey to Topaz,* which is among her more than forty published works. She wrote for children in the hope that "they can be caring human beings who don't think in terms of labels—foreigners or Asians or whatever. If that comes across, then I've accomplished my purpose."

all dressed up — + we couldn't get over seeing Pop in a white shirt. Gollee — what habit can't do, even in 4 short months.

Heard such a sad story — Mrs. Momii of S.F. passed away after an operation, father "interned" in Louisianna — came by train, with 2 guards escorting him — for the funeral." Gee, the poor kids! Heard they stuck him in the guard house for awhile — but Comm'y Welfare arr. to get him in camp — still he has to stay in Bl #1 — his guards sleep in the next room. I don't see how he can take it — poor man —

January 10, 1943

Caught my cold all over again — my d — blanket fell off — my bed! Zowie! My nose runs + runs again — so stayed home from church — Was it cold today! Brrr! —

Mom + Pop had such a swell time last nite — Pa sang Nicola, Ouchi + all! — They went to Hiro's prayer meeting — so K + I stayed home. Had company all evening —

The F.B.I. are here again — questioning all those who signed Repatriation papers — what rats!!!

stayed home from school with a lousy cold — Does my nose RUN! — Didn't do much, just puttered 'round — + read "Jr. Miss" by Sally Benson. S'was cute!

Pop had to go to a Coop meeting — didn't come home till 11:30 PM! Poor man! — Nihonjins are soooh wakarazuya

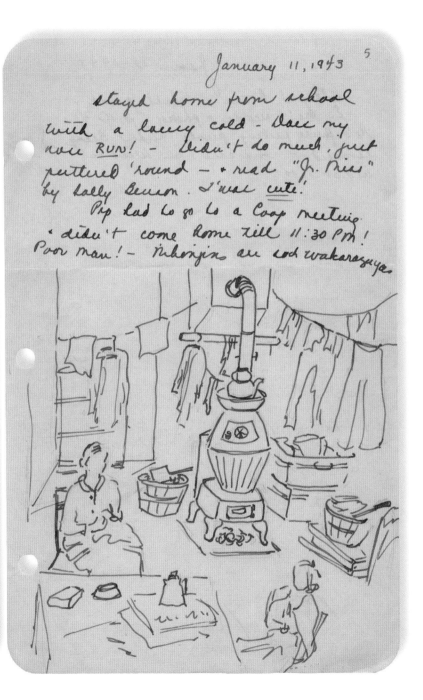

attributed to *William E. Voigt*

OCTOBER 7–OCTOBER 8, 1943

This beautifully illustrated key to magic tricks and sleight of hand, "Magic Book No. 1," may or may not have been written as a journal and may or may not have been meticulously compiled by William E. Voigt. Containing the secrets to 575 feats of magic, the diary is a well-thumbed compendium that includes photographs and clippings about admired magicians of the writer's day. As the entries progress in time, the tricks appear to progress in complexity and the tone of the writing becomes more instructional. A table of contents was appended at the end of the volume. ❖ Commercially produced blank diaries with names like Daily Record, Day by Day, and My Memoranda have been marketed for two hundred years and have provided a foundation and storehouse for thoughts, plans, records, and unvarnished me-ness.

> *"This trick is mostly for the amateur who is very inexperienced in palming. It consists of a coin, the size of a half dollar with a piece of light horse-hair attached—by a motion (circular) the coin swings to rear of hand…."*

280
Magic book 3

Thursday, October 7
280th day — 85 days follow
Holy Rosary

13 Vanishing Coin From Glass of Water

5 ½ $5

IT'S THERE

CLINK!

GONE

This trick is a very simple one. Show a half a dollar around, having palmed a piece of glass the same size — palm real coin and put glass in hkf. let spectator hold hkf. by edge of coin over a glass of water and turn loose. Motion with wand. Coin is gone.

14
½ $5
5 ¢

The Mysto Vanishing Coin

This trick is mostly for the amateur who is very inexperienced in palming. It consists of a coin, the size of a half dollar with a piece of light horse-hair attached — by a motion (circular) the coin swings to rear of hand.

281

Friday, October 8
281st day — 84 days follow

Another Good Coin Illusion 15

5 ½ $5   Hold a coin between the first and second fingers of the right hand and with your left you act as though you strip the coin out of your right hand. but realy you bend in the fingers and deposit the coin between the thumb and edge of palm edgewise (Can be made to appear in like manner) A coin in this position may be brought out from anywhere.

The Vanishing and Reappearing Half Dollar.   Best 3   16

FALSE COIN

Hold the coin between first finger and thumb of the right

hand, and place it under hkf. — Palm it and grab the one in lining. Now with left hand hold hkf. by the coin in hem and put your hand in Spectator's sholder, as you do this — drop coin in his pocket. Carry on trick in any manner you like.

Daniel Abdal-Hayy Moore

JANUARY 24, 1960

Sometimes called the poet laureate of American Islam, Oakland-born Daniel Moore was nineteen when he began keeping the first of many elaborately illuminated journals. He used his diaries as sourcebooks and as an ordering process for his writing, and they contain first drafts of much of his work, profusely illustrated with sketches and caricatures, letters, images clipped from magazines, postcards, and always poetry. In 1960, he filled the pages with sensations of chaos, feelings of angst and isolation, acute sensory perceptions, and the pain and fear of inertia, making a haven for his struggling spirit, working his way through the mire toward creative expression. His first book of poems, *Dawn Visions*, was published by Lawrence Ferlinghetti of City Lights Books four years later. Director of the Floating Lotus Magic Opera Company in Berkeley from 1966 to 1969, Moore experimented with ritual theater and dramatic poetry in productions such as "The Walls Are Running Blood" and "Bliss Apocalypse," held at the overgrown John Hinkel Park in north Berkeley. After traveling the world in his study of mystical Islam he settled in Philadelphia, eventually compiling over fifty manuscripts of poetry. In the late 1990s he revived his theatrical projects in creating the Floating Lotus Magic Puppet Theater, and he continues to give many poetry readings, often accompanying himself on a zither. His pursuit of spangled creative expression has never flagged.

DANIEL MOORE AS DEMON, 1968. PHOTOGRAPH BY BARRY OLIVIER, PHOTOGRAPHS OF THE FLOATING LOTUS MAGIC OPERA COMPANY.

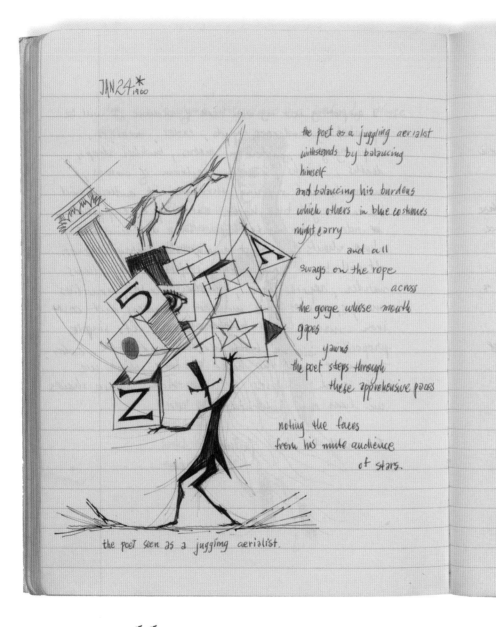

JAN 24 1900

the poet as a juggling aerialist
withstands by balancing
himself
and balancing his burdens
which others in blue costumes
might carry
                    and all
swings on the rope
                            across
the gorge whose mouth
gapes
            yawns
the poet steps through
            these apprehensive paces

noting the faces
from his mute audience
        of stars.

the poet seen as a juggling aerialist.

I am at last working on a novella. It will not be very successful, for the vision I am clothing by writing it is one of the imagination, feeling; not true, not real... But can I make this imaginative cloth, by weaving it with real thread, as real as sitting heavy in a chair, or running in the sun? Can I make illusion real, reality illusion, but so combine the two into one indivisible unity that it will achieve power and truth? Is this my taste....? I fear plunging into situations which I have only hinted at in my field of experience. Yet the vision is powerful and I wonder if I can shrug it off without completing it through the writing.. In it will be characters I know, characters I will probe until they are revealed to me, so that their speech, thought, physical realities will be shown in round form. there is an idea, one of the senses, which I feel I must clamp down on paper — It is a slow process — I am terribly unsure about it. It will be filled with mosaic episodes which fit and mesh in a seeming haphazard fashion — it will be passionate, but laconic I hope, strenuous ambiguities which will make dizziness. cabalistic unfoldings — I am blathering.

> **"** *It will be filled with mosaic episodes which fit and mesh in a seeming haphazard fashion—it will be passionate, but laconic I hope, strenuous ambiguity which will make dizziness, cabalistic unfoldings—I am blathering.* **"**

Levi Burcham

MARCH 12–MARCH 13, 1963

Born in 1912, Levi Turner Burcham studied forestry, ecology, and geography at the University of California, Berkeley, writing his dissertation, "Historical Geography of the Range Livestock Industry of California," in 1956. His career at the California Department of Forestry had him considering range improvement, watershed management, and soil vegetation studies, and from 1964 to 1966 he headed an international program of environmental research for the US Department of Defense in Washington, DC. His diaries, labeled "field notes," exhibit the same kind of ecumenical curiosity and energy. Often combining exploratory trips with exuberant family camping, he covered a wide range of topics in his entries—history, Native Californian culture, description of field, flora, and fauna—and included homespun musings and philosophy as well. The pages are interleaved with dozens of annotated and colored site maps that mark the route and stops along the way. Never dull, his diaries are full of wonder and lively interest in the surroundings, wherever they may be.

> *During the early part of the evening we observed that the level of the water in the river rose considerably. By the time we were ready to turn in, the place where we had dipped water for washing when we first arrived was several feet out in the stream and completely submerged. By morning the water level was a little below this spot. We concluded the fluctuation was due to diversions for irrigation.*

120

little below this spot. We concluded the fluctuation was due to
diversions for irrigation.

We also were given evidence of
the poor quality of the water in
the river: it has a definitely
salty taste; we used it only for
washing — ourselves and dishes — not
for cooking or drinking.

13 Mar 63
Travel: Colorado River Camp to "Windmill
Camp," in New York Mountains.

We were awake shortly after day-
break, made breakfast and packed
for the day's travel. Left our camp
at 7:45 a.m. and proceeded north on
US 95. Stopped at Vidal for gas, oil,
air, and water — filling up the two
carboys and all our canteens.

121

At Vidal Junction turned west on un-
numbered county road — paved and in
good condition — that runs from Parker
to Twenty-nine Palms

Stopped by roadside 2.6 miles (by
speedometer) west of Freda to look
and photograph —
Locality 3: Sand dunes west of Freda;
SW¼NE¼, Sec. 11, T1S, R19E, SBB+M;
San Bernardino County, California (see
Rice Quadrangle, 15 minute series).
Elevation 820 feet.

Took photos of an extensive area of
dune primrose (Oenothera deltoides
=O. trichocalyx in Jepson). Some hairy
sand verbena (Abronia villosa), a small
white-flowered "fiddleneck" (Phacelia or
Cryptantha?), and scattered clumps
of big galleta (Hilaria rigida) and
creosote bush (Larrea divaricata).
Took both close-up and general photos
of the primrose, as well as a photo
of the "bird cage" formed by the dried
stems. Had an interesting view across
the sand dunes to the Arica Mountains,

LAWRENCE FERLINGHETTI, UNIVERSITY OF ARIZONA,
OCTOBER 1967, BANCROFT PORTRAIT COLLECTION.

Lawrence Ferlinghetti

MARCH 19–MARCH 20, 1965

Lawrence Ferlinghetti: poet, editor, publisher, grand doyen and defender of the Beat poetry tradition, and founder of the iconic City Lights Books—in the words of Malcolm Margolin, "a cultural institution disguised as a business"—on the corner of Columbus and Broadway in San Francisco.

❧ In 1965 Ferlinghetti and his family lived for a couple of months in Nerja, in southwestern Spain near Seville. While there he read Orwell's *Homage to Catalonia* and Ezra Pound's poetry, studied Chinese pictographs, and observed "men with Goya faces, especially in the night streets and dim-lit bars." A man of anti-authoritarian politics, Ferlinghetti was a keen and rankled observer of post–Spanish Civil War society. His journal pages are filled with political reveries and diatribes, commentary about the state of writing and publishing during Franco's regime, and a discourse on Spanish *papel sanitario* inspired by a dark little store on the Calle de Generalísimo Francisco Franco, which appeared to sell nothing but toilet paper in variety and profusion.

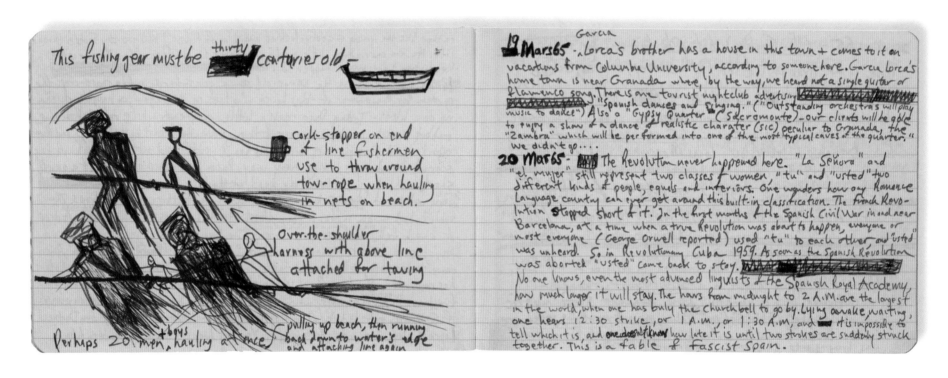

This fishing gear must be ~~thirty~~ centuries old—

Cork-stopper on end of line fishermen use to throw around tow-rope when hauling in nets on beach.

Over-the-shoulder harness with above line attached for towing

Perhaps 20 men +boys, hauling at once, pulling up beach, then running back down to water's edge and attaching line again

19 Mars 65 - Garcia Lorca's brother has a house in this town + comes to it on vacations from Columbia University, according to someone here. Garcia Lorca's home town is near Granada where, by the way, we heard not a single guitar or flamenco song. There is one tourist nightclub advertising "Spanish dances and singing." ("Outstanding orchestras will play music to dance") Also a "Gypsy Quarter" (Sacromonte) - our clients will be able to enjoy a show of a dance of realistic character (sic) peculiar to Granada, the "Zambra" which will be performed into one of the most typical caves of the quarter." We didn't go....

20 Mar 65- The Revolution never happened here. "La Señora" and "el mujer" still represent two classes of women, "tu" and "usted" two different kinds of people, equals and inferiors. One wonders how any Romance Language country can ever get around this built-in classification. The French Revolution stopped short of it. In the first months of the Spanish Civil War in and near Barcelona, at a time when a true Revolution was about to happen, everyone or most everyone (George Orwell reported) used "tu" to each other, and "usted" was unheard. So in Revolutionary Cuba 1959. As soon as the Spanish Revolution was aborted "usted" came back to stay. No one knows, even the most advanced linguists of the Spanish Royal Academy, how much longer it will stay. The hours from midnight to 2 A.M. are the longest in the world, when one has only the church bell to go by. Lying awake waiting, one hears 12:30 strike, or 1 A.M., or 1:30 A.M., and it is impossible to tell which it is, and one doesn't know how late it is until two strokes are suddenly struck together. This is a fable of Fascist Spain.

> " 21 Mar 65—I suppose generations of Spanish writers as well as Cervantes have tried to describe the sound of a burro's bellow. And unsuccessfully. It is a strangely human sound for such a loud if not raucous bellow. It has a sensitive tone, sometimes plaintive, sometimes angry or upset or impatient. It sounds most like a big hollow coal shuttle being opened and scraped with a heavy coal shovel or being shaken by its grate. At other times it's more like a huge wooden farm door being opened on loudly groaning hinges, the wood a thousand years old. Other times it sounds like a big man in a cave drunkenly trying to holler thru a bullhorn after having lost his voice. Other times it's a bull about to die, after being enraged and stuck by a bullfighter a las cinco de la tarde…I believe it is the voice of the Spanish people. "

TOP: "BUDDHA RED EARS," PHILIP WHALEN
PORTRAIT BY JACK KEROUAC, PHILIP WHALEN
PICTORIAL COLLECTION. (SKETCH)

BOTTOM: PHILIP WHALEN AND GARY SNYDER,
SHIMOYAMA, JAPAN, PHILIP WHALEN PICTORIAL
COLLECTION.

Philip Whalen

OCTOBER 18–OCTOBER 30, 1967

Attending Reed College on the GI Bill after World War II, Philip Whalen
roomed with fellow West Coast Beats Lew Welch and Gary Snyder. It
was Snyder who arranged for Whalen's several sojourns in Kyoto, Japan,
where he taught English, studied Zen Buddhism, and walked the streets
taking in the sights and sensations of the "living continuous tradition,"
and the good smells of ancient Japanese buildings and of grilled dried fish
in the early morning. His far-ranging entries on the pages of his ever-
present notebooks cover the decline of the American hot dog, the travails
of purchasing an umbrella (he ended up buying ten), the allure of jazz and
its rhythmic inventions, and meditations on St. Francis Xavier. He took
pleasure in the aggregate, the appearance of the whole page, not seeking
to "solve any problems or answer any questions." His unfolding thoughts
were expressed in his own handwriting, calligraphy, drawings, doodles, blank
space, and marginalia. This became easier when a friend introduced him to
blank books that "would take ink, paint, color, whatever," and he filled over
sixty-seven journals from 1957 to 1990. ❧ Though he bridled at the Zen
training that at one time he likened to being in the Army, he was ordained
as a monk in San Francisco in 1973. Fellow poet Dale Smith wrote that
Whalen "uses his poems as a field, or graph, on which he arranges discrete
phenomena"—an apt description of his journals as well, a many-chaptered
novel with a single main character.

18:X:67 { from looseleaf notes

Pine-tree child soaks in teapot
Chrysanthemum perfume autumn soup
and a boiling snail
That I may live forever.

28:X:67   She builds a fire of ~~small~~ ~~square~~ small clean square sticks
balanced on top of a small clay hibachi which
stands on a sewing machine set between the
house wall & the street where my taxi zooms
past.

30:X:67 2 ancient tiny ladies, dressed in dark
wadded silk kimono & jackets. One was still
beautiful. the other was older, no teeth. she
quite suddenly stood up and came across the
aisle of the streetcar to say something to
the man next to me, put something in his
hand — money? a ticket? Then she turned
to me next and gave me 3 big clear crystals
of rock candy. I thanked her, & when I was getting

off the streetcar we exchanged cheerful
bows. I wanted to give her some tiny
present in exchange, but all I had was
money in my pocket — absolutely useless &
graceless in this event. Still I felt endlessly
pleased with having met her — and felt young,
to be given candy by grandmother — & how
much more than candy: XXXXXXXXXX
hail hello love & joy across the centuries,
right through the center of the culture/
language bar &c. &c.

TRIBUTE

To Wallace Stevens.   I never should
have left the U.S.A. without copies of
all his poems.

Kim Bancroft

OCTOBER 21, 1971

Inspired by the confidential notebooks of the heroine of Louise Fitzhugh's children's novel *Harriet the Spy,* this journal was kept by a thirteen-year-old who addressed it as a stalwart and faithful friend, with steely determination to be good during a confusing time. Struggling to find her own space in a tumultuous household, she wrote in Phoenician code, exhaustively explored the rearrangement of her bedroom furniture, mapped her neighborhood, and treated every day as a new year worthy of ambitious resolutions. Sibling rivalry, a sense of isolation at school, and an intense yearning to please make for poignant pages. The precocious Bancroft used her diary as an anchor, a sounding board, a shelter for a small flame of confidence, and plain good company, but she worried that keeping a diary caused her to be more introverted than she was. If she called it a "thought book" instead of a diary, she believed it would not supersede a best friend when she found one. ❖ Bancroft and her diaries became a part of this book after she began regularly spending time in the library reading room, poring over her great-grandparents' journals, which are housed there. Library staff would see her in her favorite seat, alternately smiling and groaning as she read her family's records. It is fitting that one of her own diaries joins this multigenerational legacy.

> " *I like this book because I can look to it as a friend and a vault to my life. It does not contain all but enough to suit me fine.* "

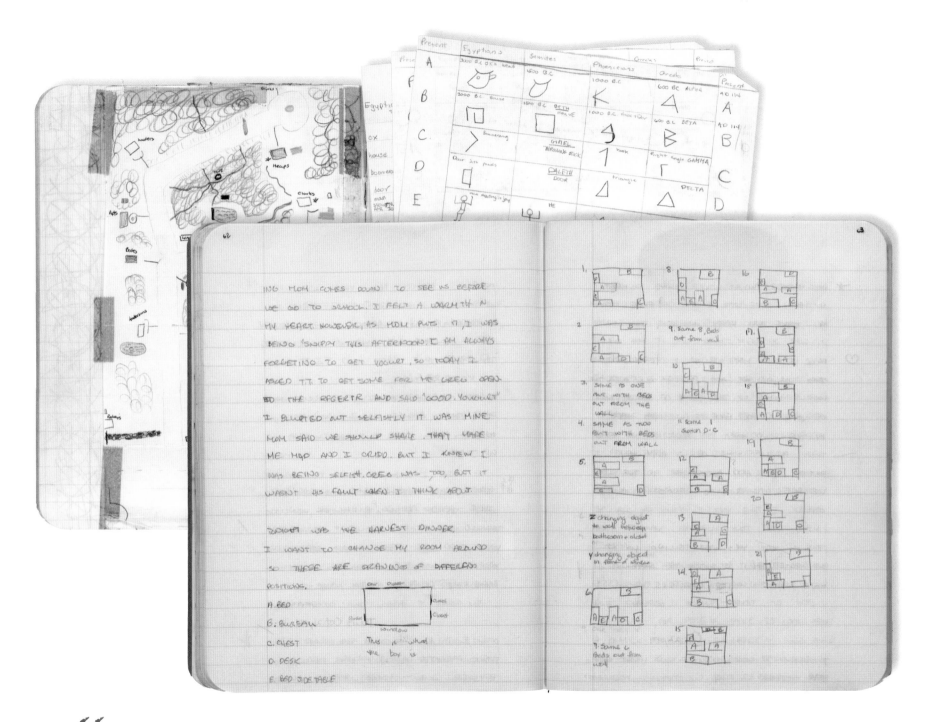

"Here I am in the doghouse. Last night I was mean. But last night is locked in so I don't need to write it. I sure am a weird teenager."

Jean Margaret Hill

FEBRUARY 1, 1973

"Where is a friend? Or why? Fresh Deliverance. Don't ya leave me here because I really want to stay too much." Coursed through by thick veins of loneliness and confusion, Jean Hill's diaries are a tribute to her stubborn determination to find "strength of mind and strength of life." When she was twenty, she went on a six-month hitchhiking tour through Europe, following whim and fancy where they led, sometimes alone and sometimes in the company of her occasional boyfriend Paul Studenski, staying in youth hostels and participating in the "incredible multicultural comradeship of youth hostellers." She was puzzled by recurrent dreams of Orson Welles, learned embroidery in Turkey in exchange for a lesson in tie-dye, slipped into US army bases for peanut butter and laundry, sold her blood for money, and wondered, "What am I doing here?" Alternately reveling in and exhausted by the "characters on the fringe" that she met and re-met as they traveled from place to place, she was often sick and strung out, depressed by one-night stands and the "insane moralistic table talk of religion and ethics" around the late-night supper tables. "Does my loneliness glow 5 hundred meters? Is it a strange magnet for so many vague individuals? Is this the only warm I have?" But she was entranced by ethnic clothing, needlework, and textiles, sought them out wherever she went, and filled her diaries with designs and patterns. She played with words and thoughts and left "Etruscan doodles" in vacant spaces, using wildly different handwriting styles from page to page. She painted word pictures with short phrases stacked one upon the other separated by dots but thought that "pictures speak better." "It was good to cook and neurotically clean the kitchen. Reality of habit. A welcome sip of lukewarm ripped-off tea. Courtesy of The Africans. Rapped at by the silly earnest Italio-Bostonian horny guy. Meditation curing the ills. Hmmm." After returning to Pasadena in May, Jean and Paul sold oddities at the weekend Rose Bowl flea market to keep themselves afloat. Just two months later, both were killed in an auto accident while driving to Paul's family reunion in Kansas.

JEAN HILL, AUGUST 1973, JEAN M. HILL PAPERS.

February 1·1973·Throat pains this morn.
Went to American Express w. high hopes
& much mail—f.i.—sketal—c'est La—Notes
from Susan, Didi + Paul's ma—500—now what.
Another pleasant day—thank God—for
this city now seems so much more city sick
than I'd remembered—like home L.A. or
someplace—there is Athens, & there is
Greece—both extremely different places—
Went to Daphni—Quite nice—style of
Mosaic less Byzantine than other stuff
A bit more conscious of realism—

XEA DOYMIA
LEGIETE LEGIETE
ORISTE! XEA DOYMIA
LEGIETE
LEGIETE
LEGIETE! SPEAK ENGLISH

about three wars ago I wondered how it
would be when the green
had all gone under from too much
influence from dirty films—probably not.

the 1st black cat moved away after
3 steps—but yet cowered close enough—
the 2nd, grey + striped flew immediately
upon my move—the 3rd—or rather
the 2nd black one scurried round behind
a tree at my fifth pace—the 4th,
large + tangerine dissapeared entirely
in response to the reaction of the
3rd—the 1st maintaining its secondary
proximity moved off upon my
retreat—the 3rd again resumed its
original spot—warm grass by tree light—

today we crushed an egg in the sack.
there it had been badly smashed
in spite of the warm protective pocket...
so we ate it...that's all...
no salt...

SEE DECEMBER 1972 issue Scientific America
on Spinning (yarn) scientific discovery as artistic
also learning in new born kittens— creation

when you're out on the road...and you
find a good place to go—always
Somebody else has been there first—

> *Today we crushed an egg in the sack—there it had been badly smashed in spite*
> *of the warm protective pocket...so we ate it...that's all...no salt...*

Ayako Miyawaki

JUNE 20, 1979

Born in 1905 in Tokyo, Ayako Miyawaki began keeping her unique journals in 1945 when her children had grown out of their babyhood and left her with time to consider how she wanted to mark her days. Using traditional homespun and well-worn fabric, easily available in the poverty of postwar Japan, she adorned each diary entry with a sketched, sewn, or collaged illustration of the

everyday objects in her world—plants in the small garden, food brought home from the market, insects, and most frequently, the fish that would later grace the dinner plate. She created a warm, loving, and industrious household with her painter husband, Haru, and would kneel in her second-story room or below by the garden, drawing, painting or assembling her daily diary entries and other appliquéd works of art—"needle art," she called it—from scraps pulled out of old baskets and dark wood chests under the staircase, noticing and giving life to the small lovely common things around her. The featured object rarely stands alone, but is accompanied by a story of its origin or travels—a leek is a gift of Gen-san that suffered from too long a stay in plastic. The Zatsugas brought her a long-legged crab and multicolored squashes from their farm. The praying mantis she

caught wouldn't stay still long enough for her to draw it, until she released it from the jar. Roots and the dirt still clinging to them, onions gone to seed, silvery dried fish in rice straw wrapping—the homely things that make a day, that speak volumes.

The Spinach that Blossomed in the Refrigerator. I can't seem to work these days. But in consolation, my house gets more and more organized with each day. Today I cleaned out the refrigerator. Scraping the ice was most troublesome. While cleaning, I thought about how I always had someone else do such tedious chores for me, and that it was a long time since I had such a good look at my own refrigerator. I felt slightly embarrassed that I was having someone else do my dirty work. But I also realized that concentrating on cleaning might be good for my health. People often tell me that I look healthy. But the fact that I can't work makes me sad.

Courtesy of Miyawaki Mihoko-san and the Toyota Museum of Art,
Toyota, Japan.

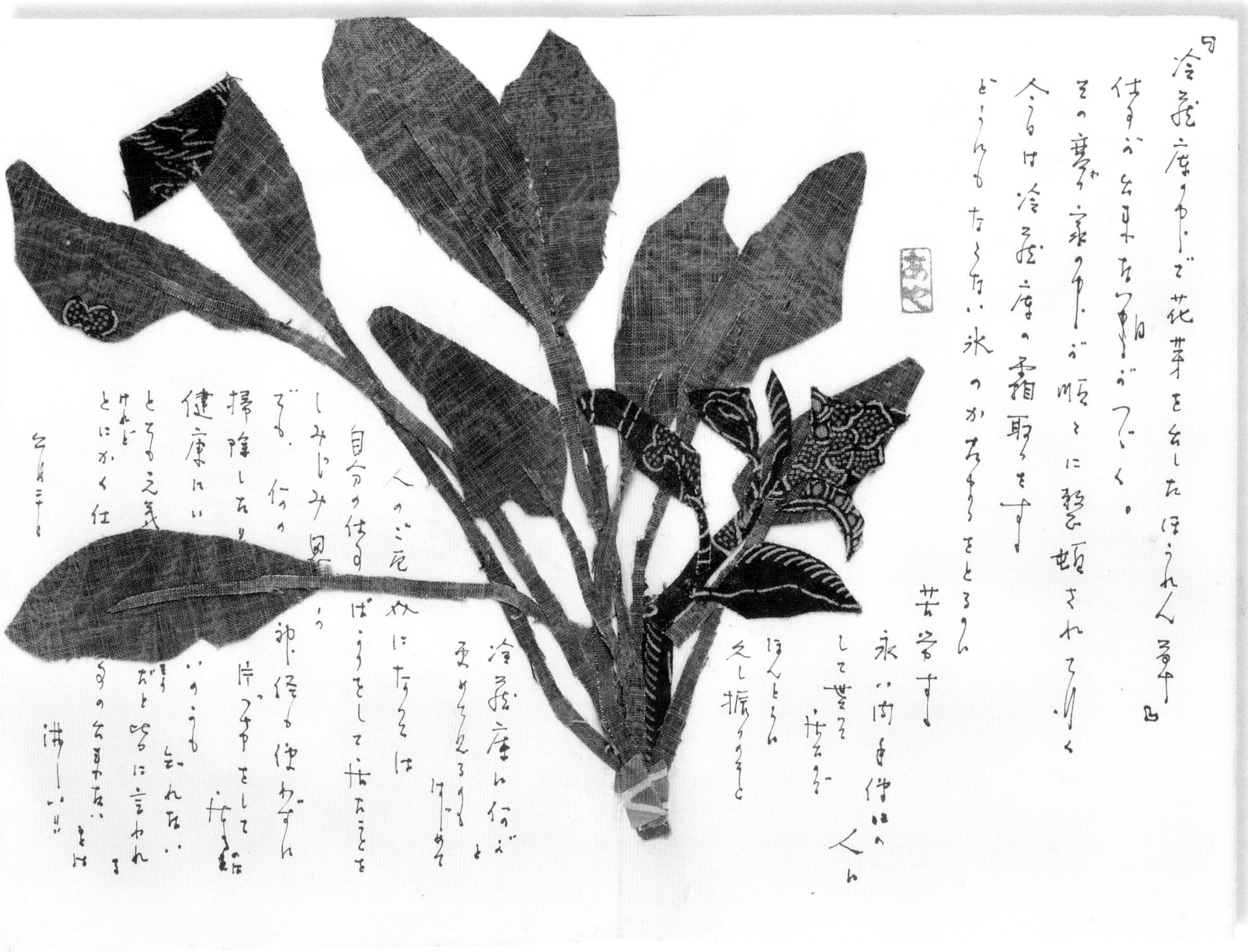
冷蔵庫の中で花芽を出したほうれん草
今日は冷蔵庫の霜取りをす
どうにもならない氷のかたまりをとる

John Brandi
1973– 1981

John Brandi was encouraged to sketch and write about what he saw and felt at a young age, when his parents gave him a box of paints to take along on road trips through the California landscape. A painter, essayist, teacher, letterpress printer, self-described "open roader," and itinerant poet, Brandi has traveled throughout the world but calls northern New Mexico home. Fellow poet and publisher Ward Abbott wrote that he "has given us the music of his inner world mixed with his clear-eyed observations of the outer world." Brandi's diaries exemplify this elixir—conversations in which both sides of the dialogue are his own, an internal cosmology, with observations of the local marketplace. Well over a hundred of his illustrated diaries document his dreamscapes, the alternately rocky and sublime terrain of his relationships, maps of himself, and the corporeal landscapes of his different sojourns, all inhabited by fish and antlered deer under magnificent weatherscapes. He delights in his vibrant colors and good paper. Each page is a work of art traversed by words in different inks in loops and slopes, intertwined with drawings, decorative borders, collage, clippings, postage stamps, tarot cards, dragonfly wings, language lessons, postcards, tickets, and an occasional hamburger wrapper. ❧ Dream diaries are a special type of journal that is dramatically enhanced by drawings of imaginary worlds. Brandi's narration of his dreamlands is as vivid as his telling of the aromatic red canyons populated by the Russian olive trees of his New Mexico home. Sir Joshua Reynolds replied, "With brains," when asked, "With what do you mix your colors, sir?" Brandi's paintings on these pages suggest a different answer: "I mix them with my heart."

" White Thorn—On the road to shelter are: the deer in the sun eating sproutings after the rain; the freaks wild hair behind huge Metro steering wheels on winding curves with the snowy peaks out of lavender mists behind, always behind. "

I was in calif. before Spaniards white
men were there ... and it was
beautiful, all around me, - beautiful!

21:III.73 after me
at Rod & Pat's
dream of
hija in the

AUND REA
CLOUD
SUNS LIPS
Rivers LI
FLOWing

vernal equinox
— a hawk
their

RAIN
FLYING
OVER A
ING
PALM
RAIN BOWS
TREES &
PALM Trees
everywhere

03:II 1:03PM

22.III.73 — I woke up and drew this
cat coming out of a smoke stack after
Rod and I walked down and crouched by
the Eel River   and realized we
were/are in   another time zone
as we watched   semis and
tourists roar   thru the red-
woods going   wood going
where? ——

white morn: — on the road to
shelter cove: the deer in the sun eating
sproutings after the rain; the peaks
wild rain behind huge Metro steering
wheels on winding curves with the snowy
peaks out of lavender mists behind, along
behind. ——
the church with the 'one way' Jesus
saves sign pointing to heaven and
Andrea gobbbling in the backseat with
giovanna asking "Do these people drive
cars?" —— Rod says, as the road turns
into dirt, "We are here but we have
somewhere else to go." —— and: have
no hinderence to one's personal development, no resistance to one's
spiritual growth: that's the idea
place.

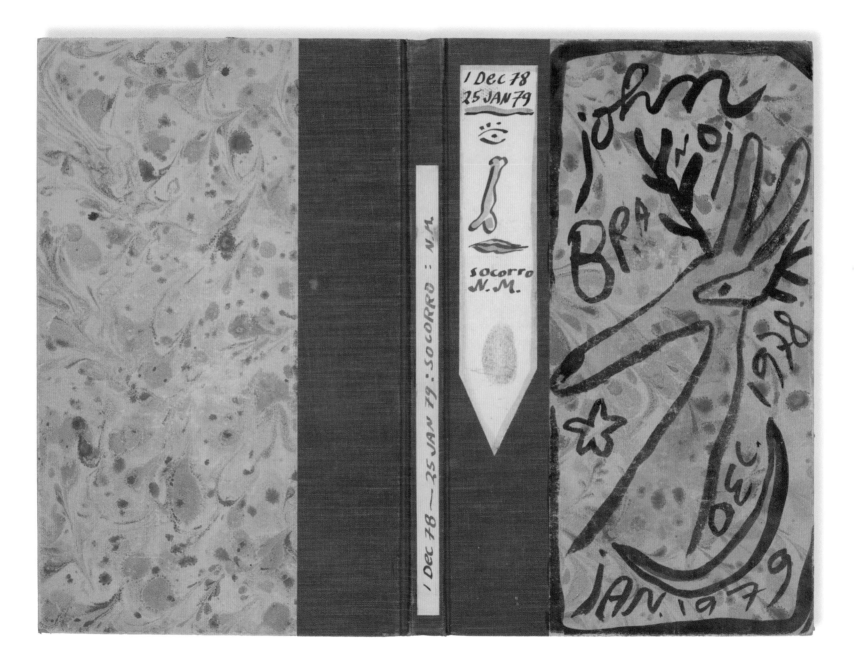

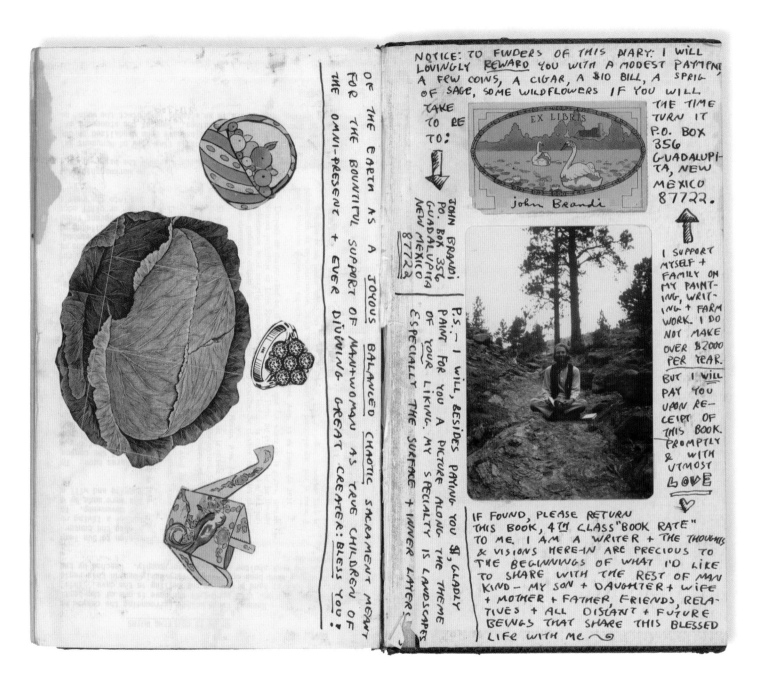

OF THE EARTH AS A JOYOUS BALANCED CHAOTIC SACRAMENT MEANT FOR THE BOUNTIFUL SUPPORT OF MANTWOMAN AS TRUE CHILDREN OF THE OMNI-PRESENT + EVER DIVIDING GREAT CREATER: BLESS YOU!

JOHN BRANDI
P.O. BOX 356
GUADALUPITA
NEW MEXICO
87722

P.S.— I WILL, BESIDES PAYING YOU $, GLADLY PAINT FOR YOU A PICTURE ALONG THE THEME OF YOUR LIKING. MY SPECIALTY IS LANDSCAPES ESPECIALLY THE SURFACE + INNER LAYERS

NOTICE: TO FINDERS OF THIS DIARY: I WILL LOVINGLY REWARD YOU WITH A MODEST PAYMENT A FEW COINS, A CIGAR, A $10 BILL, A SPRIG OF SAGE, SOME WILDFLOWERS IF YOU WILL TAKE THE TIME TO RETURN IT TO: P.O. BOX 356 GUADALUPI-TA, NEW MEXICO 87722.

EX LIBRIS
john Brandi

I SUPPORT MYSELF + FAMILY ON MY PAINT-ING, WRIT-ING + FARM WORK. I DO NOT MAKE OVER $2000 PER YEAR. BUT I WILL PAY YOU UPON RE-CEIPT OF THIS BOOK. PROMPTLY & WITH UTMOST LOVE

IF FOUND, PLEASE RETURN THIS BOOK, 4TH CLASS "BOOK RATE" TO ME. I AM A WRITER + THE THOUGHTS & VISIONS HEREIN ARE PRECIOUS TO THE BEGINNINGS OF WHAT I'D LIKE TO SHARE WITH THE REST OF MAN KIND — MY SON + DAUGHTER + WIFE + MOTHER + FATHER, FRIENDS, RELA-TIVES + ALL DISTANT + FUTURE BEINGS THAT SHARE THIS BLESSED LIFE WITH ME

Sources

The diaries pictured in *Beyond Words* are listed below with their collection numbers. All are located in The Bancroft Library, University of California, Berkeley, except: the J. D. Hawks diary, the John Muir diaries, the William Otis Raiguel diaries, the Kim Bancroft diary, the Ayako Miyawaki diary, and those of the author.

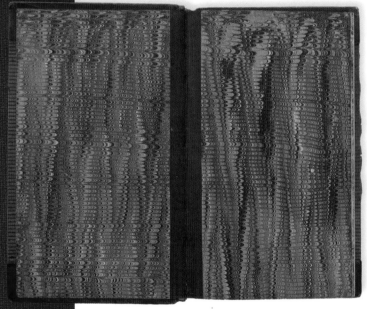

Pedro Font diary, 1776. BANC MSS M-M 1725.

Francis Phillips diary, Remarks &c. H.M.S. Racoon, 1812–1815. BANC MSS P-N 138.

Thomas Pickstock diary, 1813–1829. BANC MSS 2003/265.

William H. Meyers diary, 1841–1844. BANC MSS C-F 92 vol. 1.

Robert W. Whitworth diary, 1846–1847. BANC MSS 68/91.

George M. Hayden diary, 1846–1848. BANC MSS C-F 184 vol. 2.

Journal of a voyage from New Bedford to San Francisco, upper California, 1849. BANC MSS 77/155.

Isaac W. Baker diary, 1849. BANC MSS C-F 53 vol. 1.

J. D. Hawks diary, 1849. Alice Phelan Sullivan Library, Society of California Pioneers.

Journal of voyage of brig *Wellingsley* from Boston to San Francisco, 1849–1850. BANC MSS 2001/133.

Nelson Kingsley diary, 1849–1851. BANC MSS C-F 19.

Isaac Sherwood Halsey diary, 1849–1851. BANC MSS 79/130.

Thomas Kerr diary, 1849–1852. BANC MSS 84/36.

J. L. Akerman diary, 1854. BANC MSS 77/156.

Isaac Baker diary, 1852. BANC MSS C-F 53 vol. 2.

Robert Eccleston diary, 1853. BANC MSS C-F 47 vol. 9.

Andrew Jackson Grayson diary, 1853. BANC MSS C-B 514 box 5.

Heinrich Biedermann diary, 1854–1855, BANC MSS 99/161 vol. 3.

Stephen Wing diary, 1858. BANC MSS C-B 922 vol. 4.

William Henry Brewer field diary, 1861. BANC MSS C-B 1069 vol. 21.

Joseph LeConte diary, 1864. LeConte family papers, BANC MSS C-B 452 box 1 vol. 1.

Robert Nicholson Tate diary, 1871–1883. BANC MSS 79/98.

Caroline Eaton LeConte diaries, 1878. LeConte family papers, BANC MSS C-B 452 box 2 vol. 2 and 3

Mark Twain diary, 1879. MARK MSS 5 vol. 17.

John Muir diaries, 1867 and 1879. Holt-Atherton Special Collections, University of the Pacific.

Joshua Elliot Clayton field diary, 1879. BANC MSS P-W 27 vol. 25.

Amos Batchelder diary, 1886. Batchelder-Nelson family papers, BANC MSS C-B 614 box 1.

Mary Robertson Bradbury diary, 1886. John Galen Howard papers, BANC MSS 67/35 box 15.

Joseph Nisbet LeConte diaries, 1889 and 1890. LeConte family papers, BANC MSS C-B 452 carton 1 vols. 4 and 7.

Mae Somers Peterson diary, 1891. Mailliard family papers, BANC MSS 80/88 carton 6.

Julia Mann Barr diary, 1902. Doris Barr Stanislawski papers, BANC MSS 80/100 vol. 1.

Jessie Colmer diary, 1908–1909. BANC MSS 92/811.

Charles Royce Barney trip log, 1909–1912. Sierra Club mountain registers and records, BANC MSS 71/293 carton 2.

William Otis Raiguel diaries, 1905 and 1911. Environmental Design Archives, University of California, Berkeley, 1947-1.

Constance Topping diary, 1915–1916. BANC MSS 85/176 carton 1 vol. 2.

Florence Merriam Bailey diary, 1917. Florence Merriam Bailey papers, BANC MSS 79/139 box 6.

Russell Ray Dollarhide diary, 1917–1918. BANC MSS 2009/12.

Robert Marshall notebook, 1918. Robert Marshall papers, BANC MSS 79/94 box 14.

Charles W. Seffens diary, 1925. BANC MSS 99/174.

Death Valley automobile trip log, 1926. BANC PIC 1978.027—ALB.

Sanders Russell diary, 1926. Sanders Russell papers, BANC MSS 86/145 carton 2.

Gerald and Ina Cassidy diary, 1926. Cassidy family papers, BANC MSS 67/1 carton 1.

David Ross Brower diaries, 1928 and 1931. David Ross Brower papers, BANC MSS 79/9 box 14.

Abner Doble diary, 1931. Abner Doble papers, BANC MSS 77/183 vol. 16.

William Norris Dakin diary, 1936–1937. BANC MSS 84/181 box 1 vol. 4.

Yoshiko Uchida diaries, 1932 and 1943. Yoshiko Uchida papers, BANC MSS 86/97 box 57 and 63.

William E. Voigt magic notebook, 1943. BANC MSS 2001/54.

Daniel Abdal-Hayy Moore diary, 1960. Daniel Moore papers, BANC MSS 73/63 carton 1 vol. 1.

Levi Turner Burcham field diary, 1963. Levi Turner Burcham papers, BANC MSS 99/305 box 4.

Lawrence Ferlinghetti diary, 1965. Lawrence Ferlinghetti papers, BANC MSS 90/30 box 22.

Philip Whalen diary, 1967. Philip Whalen papers, BANC MSS 2000/93 box 1.

Kim Bancroft diary, 1971–1972. Private collection.

Jean Margaret Hill diary, 1973. Jean M. Hill papers, BANC MSS 2010/143 box 1.

Ayako Miyawaki diary, 1979. Toyota Municipal Museum of Art, Japan.

John Brandi diaries, 1973, 1977, 1981. John Brandi papers, BANC MSS 2009/112 vols. 19, 24, and 50.

august 16
Makii left for Hawai'i today. I
wanted to draw his face before
he left but there was no time.
I don't think he'll be back for
a very long time. He's gone
from me and from the way
it was and I miss him.
There is something quite final
about his leaving.

This lantana blossom was cut
when we mowed + cleaned
up the yards this afternoon.
I made several pints of pesto,
too, from basil from the
Vegetable Path. A big box
of basil. And peaches, okra,
melons: the good stuff of
high summer.

I washed sheets and towels
and cleaned up the traces of
my son. Coins of two
countries, a needle for the
ball pump, unsold text-
books, dirty clothes, crum-
pled gift wrap from an ad-
mirer.

I feel a heavy and per-
plexed sadness as if I forgot
to do something necessary
and important, and now
it's too late.

About the Author

An inveterate diarist since childhood, Susan Snyder
worked as a teacher, illustrator, and Japanese
language interpreter before becoming head of public
services at The Bancroft Library at the University
of California, Berkeley. She is the author of *Bear in
Mind: The California Grizzly* and *Past Tents: The Way
We Camped*, and coauthor of *Everyday Dogs*.

There's a mule in our midst these days—
Cana has begun to bray. Very impressive:
her Lady-Macbeth-examination of her
hands accompanied by mule sounds.
All her time is spent on standing up
but she hasn't yet learned that there
are sturdy props and improper props
and the problem is to distinguish between
the 2. Still, she's very agile and hasn't
spilled herself stiff-legged from the heights
of upright yet. The bookcases have been
discovered, as have the joy + wonder of
disembowelling them, which is fine with
me as long as the books remain reasonably
whole + dry. But why is it that she
has the most interest in the book I'm
holding, when there's a pile of bright Times
for her; in the newspaper Jim's reading when
he sets aside all the supermarket ads for
her; in the piece of clothing I'm folding
when I'm willing to give her any + all
of the unfolded ones? There has been a
quiet development that strikes me as wonderful — Cana drops a piece of bread,
it falls out of sight, perhaps under her
leg, and so she looks for it — marvelous!
And, yeah, her meals are like that - beggar's
banquets. Lunch is strictly help yourself—
and, typically, today's spot of diced potato
became mashed, + molded onto her head like a
British jurist's wig.   April 20

1

2

3

4

5

APRIL 22

The Bancroft Library

The Bancroft Library is the primary special collections library at the University of California, Berkeley. One of the largest and most heavily used libraries of manuscripts, rare books, and unique materials in the United States, Bancroft supports major research and instructional activities. The library's largest resource is the Bancroft Collection of Western Americana, which was begun by Hubert Howe Bancroft in the 1860s and which documents through primary and secondary resources in a variety of formats the social, political, economic, and cultural history of the region from the western plains states to the Pacific coast and from Panama to Alaska, with greatest emphasis on California and Mexico from the late eighteenth century to the present. The Bancroft Library is also home to the Rare Book and Literary Manuscript Collections, the Regional Oral History Office, the History of Science and Technology Collections, the Mark Twain Papers and Project, the University Archives, the Pictorial Collections, and the Center for the Tebtunis Papyri. For more information, see the library's website at http://bancroft.berkeley.edu.

*For information on the Friends of The Bancroft Library, to make
a gift or donation, or if you have other questions please contact:*

Friends of The Bancroft Library
University of California, Berkeley
Berkeley, California 94720-6000

(510) 642-3782

friends@library.berkeley.edu

Oct 7 Saturday ... Fine weather, employ'd at Sundries a
fuss kicked up, about buying plank at any other place
but the ship yard. nothing of importance occurs

8 Sunday ... mustered all hands. divinal Service
by a missionary. Text from Luke the Rich and poor man
12 dinner went on shore, at 9 returned

9 Monday ... Fine weather a number of men took
french liberty, a number taken. Complaints from the
master of the Henry Astor concerning a mutineer of his
being on board another ship, took him out, visited
by all the princes and princesses of the Royal family
about 2 doz altogether, Recreations on the Organ

10 Tuesday ... Fine weather, a lot of french liberty
men flogg'd 12 lashes each with the cats ... Saw our
extortionate bill, think there must be foul play, at
12 dinner at 4 supper at 8 reported

11 Wednesday ... fine weather 9 men a dozen each with
the cats ... a lot more took french. at 8 Reported

12 Thursday ... Fine weather flogg'd 2 men with cats
Simons and William caught. D.r ordered Simons irons
taken from his legs on account of swellings, Capt.n ordered
them kept on, requested to go on shore, Shattuck said
could not go. at 4 Supper at 8 reported

13 Friday ... Fine weather employ'd at sundries
12 dinner went on shore, at 5 P.M Knight ran
from the boat, taken a general fight, during the mauss
he stabb'd a Native in the small of the back with a
knife. at 9 returned. So ends to day

14 Saturday ... Fine weather, 30 Whalemen in the inner
harbour, 1 outside, Court on shore sentenced Knight to pay
a fine of 50 dollars and receive 100 lashes on the back
at 4 supper at 8 reported, heard that he had not a fair trial

15 Sunday ... Mustered all hands, Divine Service by
6 H I went on shore, after spending the day with
Maria, at 8 visited the Native who had been stabb.d
at 9 returned

Valley of Pali

HEYDAY
into California

ABOUT HEYDAY

Heyday is an independent, nonprofit publisher and unique cultural institution. We promote widespread awareness and celebration of California's many cultures, landscapes, and boundary-breaking ideas. Through our well-crafted books, public events, and innovative outreach programs we are building a vibrant community of readers, writers, and thinkers.

THANK YOU

It takes the collective effort of many to create a thriving literary culture. We are thankful to all the thoughtful people we have the privilege to engage with. Cheers to our writers, artists, editors, storytellers, designers, printers, bookstores, critics, cultural organizations, readers, and book lovers everywhere!

We are especially grateful for the generous funding we've received for our publications and programs during the past year from foundations and hundreds of individual donors. Major supporters include:

Anonymous; James Baechle; Bay Tree Fund; B.C.W. Trust III; S. D. Bechtel, Jr. Foundation; Barbara Jean and Fred Berensmeier; Berkeley Civic Arts Program and Civic Arts Commission; Joan Berman; Peter and Mimi Buckley; Lewis and Sheana Butler; California Council for the Humanities; California Indian Heritage Center Foundation; California State Library; California Wildlife Foundation/California Oak Foundation; Keith Campbell Foundation; Candelaria Foundation; John and Nancy Cassidy Family Foundation, through Silicon Valley Community Foundation; The Christensen Fund; Compton Foundation; Lawrence Crooks; Nik Dehejia; George and Kathleen Diskant; Donald and Janice Elliott, in honor of David Elliott, through Silicon Valley Community Foundation; Federated Indians of Graton Rancheria; Mark and Tracy Ferron; Furthur Foundation; The Fred Gellert Family Foundation; Wallace Alexander Gerbode Foundation; Wanda Lee Graves and Stephen Duscha; Alice Guild; Walter & Elise Haas Fund; Coke and James Hallowell; Carla Hills; Sandra and Chuck Hobson; G. Scott Hong Charitable Trust; James Irvine Foundation; JiJi Foundation; Marty and Pamela Krasney; Guy Lampard and Suzanne Badenhoop; LEF Foundation; Judy McAfee; Michael McCone; Joyce Milligan; Moore Family Foundation; National Endowment for the Arts; National Park Service; Theresa Park; Pease Family Fund, in honor of Bruce Kelley; The Philanthropic Collaborative; PhotoWings; Resources Legacy Fund; Alan Rosenus; Rosie the Riveter/WWII Home Front NHP; The San Francisco Foundation; San Manuel Band of Mission Indians; Savory Thymes; Hans Schoepflin; Contee and Maggie Seely; Stanley Smith Horticultural Trust; William Somerville; Stone Soup Fresno; James B. Swinerton; Swinerton Family Fund; Thendara Foundation; Tides Foundation; TomKat Charitable Trust; Lisa Van Cleef and Mark Gunson; Whole Systems Foundation; John Wiley & Sons; Peter Booth Wiley and Valerie Barth; Dean Witter Foundation; and Yocha Dehe Wintun Nation.

BOARD OF DIRECTORS

GETTING INVOLVED

To learn more about our publications, events, membership club, and other ways you can participate, please visit www.heydaybooks.com.

Saturday . . . . Fine weather, employed at Sundries

. . . kicked up, about buying plank at any other pla

at the ship yard. nothing of importance occur

Sunday . . . mustered all hands. dismal Service

of a missionary. Text from Luke the Rich and poor

2 dinned went on shore at 9 returned

Monday . . . Fine weather a number of men too

french liberty, a number taken. Complaints from the

Master of the Henry Astor concerning a mutineer of

being on board another ship, took him out, visit

all the princes and princesses of the Royal Fam

about 2 doz altogether, Recreations on the Organ

Tuesday . . . . Fine weather, a lot of French libert

men flogg'd 12 lashes each with the cats . . . Saw oi

extortionate bill, think there must be foul play, a

2 dinned at 4 Supper at 8 Reported

Wednesday . . . . Fine weather 9 men a dozen each